T ARTICLES OF VIRTU·

SILVER

SILVER

Edited by Philippa Glanville

Victoria and Albert Museum

First published by the Victoria and Albert Museum, London, 1996

The Victoria and Albert Museum
London SW7 2RL

© The Board of Trustees of the Victoria and Albert Museum 1996

Philippa Glanville asserts her moral right to be identified as author of this book.

Designed by Bernard Higton

ISBN: 1 85177 172 7 (hardback)

A catalogue record for this book is available from the British Library.

Jacket illustration, front and back:
Epergne dressed in contemporary style with fruits, London 1764–65,
mark of Thomas Pitts (V&A M.1703-1944)
Front flap: Monkey Spoon, painted enamel on silver, Franco-Flemish
mid-15th-century (V&A C.2-1935)
Back flap: electrotype lion taken from the original silver models at
Rosenborg Castle, Denmark, about 1885 (V&A 1885-194&a)

Printed in Hong Kong, by South Sea International

CONTENTS

ACKNOWLEDGEMENTS

We are grateful to the following for their assistance with this publication:
The Goldsmiths' Company, especially David Beasley;
The Fishmongers' Company; David Wickham,
The Clothworkers' Company; Michèle Bimbenet-Privat, Archives
Nationales, Paris; John Evans, J.W. Evans & Sons Ltd., Birmingham;
L.B. Gans; Ivan Katzen; Clare Walsh, Department of Design,
University of Teesside; and Jessica White, The British Museum.

Thanks are also due to John Styles, V&A/RCA course leader; members of
Metalwork Conservation and Nigel Blades of the Science Section;
Douglas Payne, Friend of the V&A; and Madeleine Tilley and
Louise Hofman, Metalwork, Silver and Jewellery Department
Many thanks are due to Mary Butler for her patience and to
Amelia Fearn whose dedication has ensured the completion of this book.
All photographic credits are acknowledged on pages 132–136.

INTRODUCTION

Money spent on strong substantial plate will do you more good than in your purse.

A MOTHER'S ADVICE TO HER SON, 1630.

A theme running through this account of silver is that it was never solely a rich man's pleasure. Silver has a universal appeal and a powerful hold on the imagination; for century after century it was the necessary luxury. Until recently, it had little competition for the principal social rites of eating and in particular drinking and is still without rival for use in worship and ceremony. Lustrous, gleaming, durable, pure and without taint, conferring honour and expressing status, capable of being refashioned again and again, no other material has the qualities of silver. The only exception is gold, which has always been rarer and more costly, and is most often found as a thin imitative coating on silver (gilding).

Silver provided an instantly convertible reserve of wealth, the value of which lay in the metal rather than the workmanship: Charles I, needing to pay his troops defending Newark in 1646, could leave behind his dinner plates and dishes to be cut up into crude shillings. It has left a richer paper-trail than any other material, since owners, corporate or private, took the precaution of weighing and recording every piece. In order to keep control of large numbers of valuable objects, owners often stamped or engraved silver with marks of ownership or at least a 'scratch weight'. Silver was weighed in Troy ounces (oz. and dwt., one ounce is equivalent to approximately 31 grams) and penny weights and this ancient system, now abandoned, is the basis of goldsmiths' bills, inventories and other plate records. A complex system of alphabets and symbols – moryon heads, hearts, globes – were 'stryken' on to Henry VIII's vast collection of Scullery plate for his many palaces, in order to help the household clerks keep track of it. Despite their care, thousands of ounces went missing over the years, for which the clerks' widows were held accountable. Silver was borrowed or hired for entertaining on a large scale and a careful check was made on its return. The cancellations and annotations on the page listing dining silver lent in 1768 are characteristic of the records kept by the Jewel House. There are large gaps in the documentation in the mid-seventeenth century because the Master of the Jewel House did not wish to be held responsible for the plate that had disappeared from his charge during the Civil War and Commonwealth.

As an enduring symbol of wealth, silver has inevitably attracted the attention of the taxman since ancient times. In 1291 and in 1758 the English Crown introduced a tax on plate holdings and the well-known and much-regretted rarity of important French silver is directly attributable to Louis XIV's campaigns against plate ownership. Taxes on new plate by weight, introduced in England by George I, created the phenomenon of the 'duty dodger', in which marks cut from an older object were soldered into something new and weighty, such as in the Warrington Fountain at the Goldsmiths' Company. After the Second World War, under George VI, the luxury tax on new plate became so onerous as almost to stifle the revival of the English trade.

Silver has one special and ancient attribute. Like gold, its unique and intimate relationship with currency necessitated the oldest form of consumer protection, guaranteeing the consistency of the alloy, the mixture of pure silver and base metals in various

Silver lent by the Jewel House for a royal dinner in 1768.
Three spoons were lost.

proportions. Testing and marking the purity of precious metals has a continuous history in north-western Europe of more than seven centuries. This bedrock of certainty around the precious metals has eaten deep into our consciousness and explains the persistence of proverbs and phrases triggered by the process of assay. Expressions such as 'good as gold', 'sterling standard' or 'hallmark quality' retain a resonance even when exploited and debased by advertisers. To have been 'tried and tested' means to have been found pure, reliable and true just as a vessel of unknown composition would be sampled (assayed and tested by cupellation). To 'go through the fire' refers to the process whereby a

vessel was melted in a furnace to yield up its precious content, gleaming amongst the dross. A touchstone is a known standard of quality used to test something uncertain, just as it has been for goldsmiths since the Middle Ages. Other attributes of the precious metals have entered the language. Perhaps the classical epithet 'silver-tongued' carries a hint of disapproval and to be 'born with a silver spoon in the mouth' indicates advantages that are innate rather than earned. Rolls Royce chose carefully when it named its standard model the Silver Ghost, powerfully combining associations that are deeply embedded. At the time of writing the English hallmarking system, with a continuous history since 1300, is under threat from Brussels. The requirement that any article of silver offered for sale in the United Kingdom has to conform to the sterling standard is regarded by the German and Italian industries as a restriction on trade.

The purity of silver is both proverbial and actual. It is sterile, or rather anti-bacterial, a property appreciated if not understood scientifically by apothecaries, surgeons and nurses since the Middle Ages and now exploited in an innovative dressing for burns containing silver. The Knights of St John of Jerusalem equipped each bed in their grand hospital in Valletta with a silver bowl, cup and spoon and well-equipped nurseries had silver papboats, 'sucking bottles' and spoons for feeding infants. In the colonnade of the Amber Palace in Jaipur stands a pair of massive four-handled silver water pots which travelled with the Maharajah to ensure a supply of pure water for ritual and hygienic purposes. The cleanliness of silver linked to its efficient heat transmission made it a practical material in the kitchen. A silver saucepan, kettle or chafing dish heats up fast and uniformly, and cookery books recommended silver utensils for shredding lettuce, steeping apricots in syrup and stirring milk and egg dishes.

A famous or notorious attribute of silver is its supposed efficacy against enchantment. Silver bullets are thought to have a unique power over the familiars of witches. As recently as 1989 one of President Ceausescu's death squad in Romania claimed to a BBC reporter to have taken the precaution of substituting one. It may sound far-fetched, but this long-standing belief was the basis of a political cartoon in the *Guardian* newspaper in 1995 (about the survival of the Prime Minister John Major). In Lincolnshire within living memory a veterinary surgeon found himself unsuccessfully matching skills with a white witch whose armoury included a silver bodkin. A scratch with this counteracted a wasting spell.

Silver is virtually indestructible and can be reclaimed and reworked with little loss whatever disaster occurs. Unlike gold, which is valuable and portable even in small amounts, hoards of silver are bulky and have often been concealed to await safer times. The Danish nation has benefited from a far-sighted law on treasure trove passed in the mid-seventeenth century, which has kept together fascinating discoveries of domestic and liturgical plate. Lost treasures have been recovered by boys out ferreting and by mudlarks using metal detectors. Marine archaeologists are at present seeking the silver of Charles I that was lost when a ferry capsized crossing the Firth of Forth in 1633. For art historians, the excitement lies in the possibility of illuminating the taste of this connoisseur king, glimpsed in contemporary inventories and a handful of extraordinary objects. For the press and public, it is the lure of treasure reclaimed that makes headlines. These two attitudes can be seen at work in the incident of Cnut's great gilt cross, destroyed in the siege of Hyde Abbey in Winchester in 1141. The Bishop of Winchester used the opportunity to pay off his troops with the 60 marks of gold and more than 500 marks of silver salvaged from the ashes, but the memory of this beautiful and massive work of art was preserved by the chroniclers.

For many centuries most new silver objects had to be made by melting down old. The silver mines of the ancient world were virtually exhausted and most European mines produced only a trickle of silver as a by-product of lead and tin. The plate of the Duke of Norfolk, seized in 1571, weighed more than the entire production of the Aberystwyth mines a generation later and 50 to 60 ounces of silver (a good-sized cup) was regarded as a good yield from a tonne of Welsh tin in the late seventeenth century. When the silver deposits

London milkmaids hired silver and danced before their customers' doors to attract gifts.

at Potosi in Peru were seized and exploited by the Spanish in 1545, the English and other northern Europeans were already enjoying the dramatic release of precious metals accumulated by the Church over 900 years. It is no coincidence that after the Reformation more people owned silver than ever before. Consistently in English inventories 10 per cent of those in the lowest social groups left some silver, however small ('my salt for a poor remembrance') and higher in society silver flowed into livery halls and colleges, as well as private hands.

For public expressions of worship or ceremony, objects must be visible at a distance. Silver, which reflects so beautifully, looks better by the glancing, flickering light of candles or a fire than by the even glare of electricity. It has a powerful attraction, even out of doors. The milkmaids of London, dancing on May Day morning in their finery and carrying on their heads towers of silver, had both the clinking metal and the flashing sunlight to catch the attention of their customers. A saint's day procession with crosses, statues and candelabra glinting in the sun is a powerful magnet for devout thoughts. An exhibition in 1994 of Augsburg silver reassembled goldsmiths' work made for the court chapel with *Wunderkammer* pieces and silver furniture for state and private apartments, vividly recapturing the drama and sheer visual power of these splendid objects.

The aesthetic potential of silver, as the illustrations in this book show, is enormous. Silver can be chased, pierced, cast, enamelled, gilded and shaped with extraordinary complexity. From foil or braid to the life-size lions guarding the throne of the Danish monarch, its applications have been limited only by human ingenuity in devising and working it. From a fifteenth-century Flemish artist to Ben Nicholson, artists have enjoyed the challenge of depicting the precious metals, expressing in their rich reflective surfaces a complex mix of symbolic and painterly messages. For patrons, a painting might be a record of a treasured object or a vanitas evoking more complex emotions.

Since the 1890s, there has been a dramatic shift in the long English love affair with silver. In 1914 there were over 90 silver and jewellery businesses in London between the Strand and the City. In 1900 the Birmingham, Sheffield and London assay offices assayed and marked more than 186,000 kilograms (six-and-a-half million ounces of Troy silver). A century later the Sheffield office has closed and London and Birmingham are handling a fraction of this workload, most of it silver jewellery rather than plate.

Old silver is still valued, passed on, collected and admired in museums and treasuries. Auctions and fairs are well publicized, the Antiques Road Show attracts as many viewers as the National Lottery (13 million plus) and objects fetching high prices at auction are considered newsworthy. But at home, silver is no longer generally seen as either a necessity or a pleasure. The aspiration to give and receive plate as a wedding present and to use it on the dining- or tea-table has largely evaporated and the traditional manufacturing trade is in terminal decline. But there is a phenomenon in the British Isles, a resurgence of activity in small workshops,

encouraged by the Goldsmiths' Company and the Crafts Council. More than a quarter of the population regularly attends craft fairs and the seven colleges offering BA honours degrees in silversmithing are oversubscribed. The inventive and quirky designs of English silversmiths are admired overseas, as is their willingness to experiment with new materials and more economical methods of production, such as electroforming. Leading silversmiths not only seek out overseas orders but also design in other media. Good modern silver is invisible in the traditional high-street shops but sells well in museum or craft shops.

Security, cleaning and impracticality are the perceived negative aspects that explain the disappearance of the traditional middle market for new silver. The illusion that silver represents a store of great value is deeply cherished in England, and was reinforced by Bunker Hunt's manipulation of the meltprice in 1980. For centuries this was true. Until 1920 a coin contained almost its value in silver. Today, a burglar can probably raise more cash more quickly with a CD player than with a Victorian tea service, which may be identified by its marks, can be passed on for only a fraction of its insurance value and is worth little even at its official meltprice. And yet, the latter is somehow seen as special and worthy of preservation even if it is unusable and lives under the bed or in a deposit box. It would be better for the craft and more enjoyable for the owner if antique silver were sold and something new created, perhaps to become a treasure in its own right. This was always the practice in the past. Silver reflected its time and gave pleasure, and was then melted down without sentiment and refashioned into something else. The metal is cheaper in real terms than it has ever been (less than £4 an ounce) and, in any case, who counts the cost of the raw materials of an oil painting? It is the art that encapsulates the value.

Above: Touchneedles tipped with metal of a known standard were used to test doubtful silver

As far as cleaning is concerned the difficulty is greatly exaggerated. The effort of cleaning a complete dinner service is likely to be an issue only for those with the means to employ servants. For flatware in daily use, cleaning should not be more than an occasional necessity. The arrival of brilliant electric light a century ago has had much to do with the passion for shiny silver, which would be regarded as overcleaned by our ancestors. Silver is far better seen by candlelight when its reflective gleam and dissolving lustre can be enjoyed. A little tarnish merely adds contrast.

In the past century and a half many books on silver have been written. Some authors have been concerned with craft history, some with the history of design and some with the social history of the metal. Since the early years of the national collection of silver at the Victoria and Albert Museum in the 1850s, fashions in collecting have constantly fluctuated. At one time elaborate objects of the sixteenth century were admired, at another the plain geometry of the early eighteenth century, and it is only in the past 30 years that silver of the Rococo and the late nineteenth century has been fully appreciated. Our intention here is to offer an overview of contrasting aspects of the design, craft and social history of silver. We have suggested further reading, and listed collections in Britain and overseas, in the hope of stimulating a wider understanding of this fascinating and ancient metal.

The innovative use of colour in this contemporary piece by Kevin Coates disguises the expected white or gilt of silver.

—I—

DESIGN AND CONTEXT

The Mérode Cup, Flemish, about 1400, silvergilt with inset *plique-à-jour* enamel.

THE MIDDLE AGES

It is hard for us now to comprehend the importance of precious metal in the Middle Ages and its significance in the imagination and aspirations of the time. The economic and social gulfs were extreme: where a commoner or ordinary person in the fifteenth century might survive on a silver penny a week, great men and women lived in conspicuous ostentation of wealth. One of the richest men of his day, Duke Philip the Good of Burgundy, son of the King of France, was worth an estimated two million gold écus on his death in 1467 and this was regarded by his court chronicler as both impressive and natural. The public display of riches in the form of jewellery, gold and silver plate (often embellished with gems and enamel) was an essential indicator and attribute of status and power.

Magnificence was expected of medieval monarchs and nobles. In the royal courts of Europe there was hardly an event that was not made the occasion for the presentation of gifts, usually of gold, silver and gems. Betrothals, marriages, births, banquets, the welcoming of emissaries and ambassadors, ceremonial entry into a town by a prince or princess – all served as occasions for the giving or exchanging of presents.

Present-giving was a formalized ritual in which gifts were carefully graded according to rank and to some extent standardized. A silver cup and cover was the usual reward of an English king for visiting envoys in the fourteenth century, but by the 1430s the Burgundian dukes were giving a silvergilt ewer and six beakers. New Year was the most important annual occasion for present-giving, when elaborate gifts of plate and jewellery were exchanged by members of royal and noble families; courtiers, leading officials and retainers received gifts of lesser value. In 1398 Richard II of England was included in the French royal New Year circle, and received from the Duke of Burgundy the most valuable present (after that given to the Duchess): a gold and ruby image of his patron, St Edmund.

Splendid feasts were an indispensable expression of power on the part of medieval monarchs and noblemen, who would eat in state even when dining alone. Plate would be displayed on tiered 'buffets' or cupboards (that is, boards to hold cups). The grandest royal banquets usually had several plate-laden buffets, at least one of which was entirely for show, 'to make men Marvel', according to the court chronicler Chastellain. The account of the splendid feast held by Philip the Good in 1456 at the Hague, for his chivalric Order of the Golden Fleece, describes a hall hung with tapestries depicting the tale of Jason. Of the three buffets, one bore silver vessels for the ordinary guests, one had silvergilt vessels for the knights, and one held gold and gem-encrusted vessels for show. The room beside the banqueting hall was heaped with silver plate, and all who wanted could go and see it, 'showing that even if the Duke lacked coin he had the means of making it'.

Silver was the principal basis for all European coinage throughout the Middle Ages. In an age without banks, plate and jewellery represented bullion as well as beauty, and in a crisis magnates could easily sell what they had amassed or melt it down for coin. The regulation of the purity of silver and the working practices of goldsmiths, who handled both silver and gold, were therefore matters of the greatest importance to

One of a set of eight enamel plaques made in France around 1350.

the ruling powers. The sterling standard of 92.5 per cent purity was the rule in France and England, although it was often broken for silver coin and plate. (The term 'sterling' originates from the name for the silver English penny of the eleventh century.) Elsewhere in Europe different standards prevailed, but, by the end of the Middle Ages, most goldsmiths were strictly regulated and various marking systems in place.

Because so much has been destroyed, any study of medieval plate relies heavily on descriptions in written sources. Surviving examples of medieval plate are very rare; spoons and drinking vessels predominate. However, from contemporary inventories we learn of the huge quantities of gold and silver that were in use in noble and royal European households from the thirteenth century onwards: jugs and basins, salt cellars and wine-fountains, as well as cups and spoons. There can be little doubt that the average goldsmith spent more time supplying these than providing for the Church's needs. Apart from making new pieces, the goldsmith had constantly to repair damaged ones, or to remodel them entirely to a more fashionable shape. The Romanesque and Gothic styles dominant in architecture between about 1050 and 1520 influenced goldsmiths and their clients. The Ramsey Abbey

censer of about 1325 is shaped like a miniature chapter house in the 'Decorated' style, and the Mérode Cup has enamels inspired by Gothic stained glass.

The Victoria and Albert Museum has two exceptionally rare fifteenth-century pieces that must have been intended for display rather than use: the silver 'Monkey' spoon (see 'Spoons') and the Mérode Cup. Both are embellished with delicate enamel and were probably made in Flanders for the royal court. Spoons decorated with this sort of enamel are known from the inventories of the great fourteenth-century patron of the arts Jean, Duc de Berri, brother of Charles V of France, but this is the only one known to survive. The Mérode Cup is also of great technical interest as it is the earliest example of this type of enamel.

The serpentine ewer mounted in silvergilt might perhaps have been intended for use as well as display. Goldsmiths used precious and semi-precious stones and rarities like coconut shell to add exoticism as well as value to their products. Some stones were believed to have amuletic or protective powers: it was understood that crystal, for instance, provided protection from poison.

A notable contrast with such display pieces is provided by the simple vessels in the French enamelled plaque of the Last Supper. The plate consists of bowls (the larger ones for fish and lamb), chalice-shaped cups and knives. A modern eye will notice the absence of spoons, forks, plates and glasses. At that time plates were unknown; their function was usually performed by trenchers made of very thick slices of stale bread or pieces of wood. Forks were used only occasionally for delicacies like green ginger. Glasses were a rarity; drinking vessels consisted either of beakers (plainer versions of the Mérode Cup), chalice-shaped cups or bowls, which were sometimes used communally.

Bowls might be made of precious metal or wood mounted with silver. Mazer wood (from Old High German *masa* meaning 'spot'), a burr grown by the maple tree, was often used for these bowls. This wood is particularly suitable for vessels subject to tension from being alternately wet then dry because, as it has no grain, it is not liable to shrink and split. The distinctive wide and shallow shape of mazer bowls was determined by the natural form of maple burrs; the disadvantage of shallowness was overcome by mounting the bowls with broad lips to give additional depth. Further decoration

often took the form of a 'print' or roundel of silver or enamel set into the bottom of the bowl.

It seems likely that the shape of mazers influenced that of wholly silver drinking bowls made by goldsmiths. All four bowls from the fourteenth-century Rouen treasure in the Victoria and Albert Museum were probably used for drinking. In profile they resemble both mazers and the bowls on the enamel panel. The Rouen treasure, which consists almost entirely of drinking bowls and spoons, is a classic hoard hidden, perhaps centuries ago, and discovered only comparatively recently in 1864. Items from it are now spread between the Victoria and Albert Museum and museums in Paris and St Petersburg.

The horn was a distinctively northern form of drinking vessel used by Franks, Scandinavians and Anglo-Saxons. It is depicted on the eleventh-century Bayeux tapestry and was still in use in some countries in the seventeenth century. The Middle English text on one of the silver mounts on the Pusey Horn commemorates a grant of land to the Pusey family by King Cnut.

The Pusey Horn is by tradition a gift from King Cnut to William Pusey.

of St Edward the Confessor at Westminster Abbey, St Thomas à Becket at Canterbury and St Edmund at Bury. All were destroyed in the 16th century.

Reliquaries, containers for minor relics, either took architectural forms or were shaped to the part of the body enclosed. In an exact religious counterpart to the secular practice of displaying plate, late medieval churches organized formal displays of relics and their precious reliquaries on holy days and during Holy Week.

The shrine of St Edmund of East Anglia at Bury St Edmund's Abbey, before which Henry VI of England is shown kneeling, was much visited by English monarchs over the centuries until it was destroyed during the Reformation. It is recorded that the shrine containing his body was covered with gold, silver and gems.

Its Latin inscription indicates that this candlestick was given by Peter Abbot of Gloucester to St Peter's Abbey between 1107 and 1113. The central knop shows the symbols of the Evangelists but otherwise the ornament seems entirely secular. This masterpiece of the metal sculptor's art is made of a ramshackle alloy of silver, copper, iron, lead and arsenic, a combination forbidden to later goldsmiths.

Gold and silver have been linked with the rituals of religious practice since ancient times as their purity and value symbolize the divine. As expressed in the Old Testament, 'the words of the Lord are unalloyed; silver refined in a crucible, gold purified seven times over' (Psalms 12: 6).

The increasing prosperity throughout Europe from about 1050 to 1300 led to a revival of building on a large scale, especially of cathedrals and churches. Demand for church vessels was stimulated as the Church, always a steady customer for goldsmiths, needed plate for the Mass (chalices, cruets, pyxes, paxes, monstrances) and for other liturgical and sacred purposes (crosses, crosiers, candlesticks, altarpieces and reliquaries).

The grandest and most costly commissions were the shrines to contain the bodies, bones or other relics of the saints and martyrs. These shrines, up to two metres in length, were usually made of wood and covered with gold, silver, gems and enamels. They often depicted scenes from the life of Christ and that of the saint in question. At first, in the Romanesque period (about 1050–1210), shrines were sarcophagus-shaped with rounded niches and statuesque figures. The Three Kings shrine in Cologne Cathedral of about 1170–1230 (see 'Ceremony and Authority'), one of the earliest and certainly the largest of all medieval shrines to survive, is such an example. From the first decade of the thirteenth century, under the influence of the Gothic style, shrines evolved to resemble churches with painted Gothic arches. Most cathedrals in England had a shrine dedicated to their patron saint. Three of the most important were those

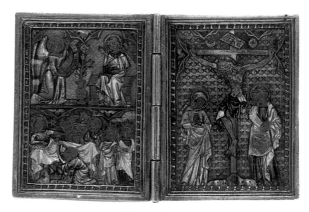

This tiny miniature altarpiece used for private prayer is enamelled on both sides. Its original owner probably had a particular devotion to Saints Christopher and George, whom it depicts with scenes from the life of Christ.

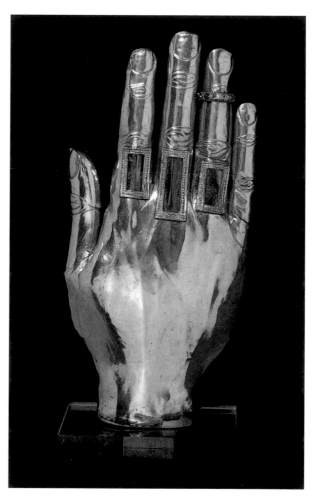

Christian de Hondt Abbot of Ter Duingen (1495–1509), is here shown with his symbols of office, his crosier and mitre, both adorned with silver and gems. The collection of silver jugs and vessels on his cupboard and the numerous rings on his fingers indicate his wealth and high status.

The bones of venerated saints were often housed in appropriately formed reliquaries. The bones of the unknown saint (now lost) would have been visible through the windows on the fingers of this reliquary.

This chalice was already old when it was buried as a token of office in the grave of Archbishop Hubert Walter in 1205. Engraved with complex blossoms typical of English Romanesque ornament, it is the most elaborate early medieval English chalice known.

RENAISSANCE

Although the Italians are credited with the revival of Classical forms and with the origination of the *mélange* of concepts and visual imagery that we now call the Renaissance, it was in the Germanic cities and, especially, in Flanders and France that the range of ornamental motifs was developed most creatively. It was here that ideas from chivalry were incorporated and plate produced 'in the new fashion' for a wide market. By 1530 the Renaissance was formally established in the repertoire of northern European goldsmiths and a new vocabulary of widely recognized motifs – antique, grotesque, arabesque, damascene, winged boys – were familiar both to patrons and to inventory clerks. The decoration of plate commissioned by patrons continued largely to be dictated by heraldry or other personal references. The 1561 inventory of William Herbert, the Earl of Pembroke, has the following entry for 'a pair of flagons fair chased having escutcheons of my lords arms on each side in garters with a green dragon in the top with bearing a flagon chain.'

Splendour was a princely obligation. There was an almost liturgical dignity to the public acts of rulers as they constantly strove to build up their holdings of goldsmiths' work by gift or confiscation. 'Curiously wrought' was a term of high praise, and novelty and inventive design were all important. This was particularly true in relation to court plate, as Queen Elizabeth stressed in her instruction about a present of plate for the Sultan. Goldsmiths were under pressure to create intricate, lavishly decorated ensembles, such as the Paris salt of about 1530 which incorporates that innovation, a clock, as well as 'antique' busts in hardstone.

This marriage of a fashionable piece of technology with Classical motifs, presumably a diplomatic gift, was in Henry VIII's collection.

The Jewel House of Henry VIII, not one of the richest of the European princes, contained about 1,000 sets of entries of goldsmiths' work at the time of his death in 1547. Apart from the regalia and some named mid-fifteenth-century standing salts (the Two Fools, the Morris Dance and the Shepherd), few of the objects pre-dated his father's time and many had come to his hands in 1530 from Cardinal Wolsey's collection. Wolsey had a keen eye for goldsmiths' work: he treasured the gold cups given to him by Francis I at the Field of the Cloth of Gold, ordered plate from Bruges and admired the new 'antique' style. Henry's plate, which he built up from some 800 sets in 1521, had largely vanished by 1574, swept into the melting pot because it was out of fashion or given away.

As during the Middle Ages, the reason for the massive accumulation of goldsmiths' work was three-fold: to demonstrate standing and wealth, to support external relationships and to act as a store of value for hard times. For a prince the obligation to show his munificence extended to presenting foreign envoys on departure with a complete service of silvergilt as well as sending plate for use during the visit. For a corporation or a guild, goldsmiths' work acquired as gifts was lent for royal visits or civic banquets. It could also be sold to pay taxes or invest in property, as the London Vintners' Company did in the 1540s.

Following the etiquette of the Burgundian court, a dinner was judged by the size and height of the buffets of plate and whether the vessels on display were made

Opposite: A rich 'cloth of gold' and a buffet of silver and gilt plate dominate this early 16th-century dining scene.

of gold or less costly silvergilt. The chronicler Edward Hall described how Henry VIII publicized his wealth and taste by leaving on show to the public at Greenwich for three or four days the seven-stage buffet dressed with gold vessels for the visit of French ambassadors in May 1527 so 'that all honest persons might see'. The statement that 'the basins were so massye that they troubled sore the bearers' is not likely to be hyperbole, given that Henry's Jewel House in 1549 included at least one basin set with gem stones that weighed more than 17 kilos, hard for a servant to manipulate gracefully for the handwashing ceremony at the end of dinner.

How were the new visual vocabularies disseminated so rapidly and so widely? The simple answer is through the printing press and engravers' shops. Designs could easily be carried as printed sheets, in sketchbooks assembled by journeymen travelling from one centre to another or in the form of lead or boxwood patterns. Some of the latter survive in Basle, in the collection of the humanist Basilius Amerbach, along with early sixteenth-century workshop drawings for cups and dinner plate. Such drawings as the designs by Giulio Romano for the Mantuan court were copied because their inventiveness was admired. Some rulers who admired the new aesthetic encouraged the copying of designs. Margaret, Duchess of Savoy and Governor of the Netherlands for Charles V, had a policy of sending the best Flemish artists to Italy to expose them to the fountainhead. Goldsmiths and engravers intermarried and worked closely together, developing their collective skills through their common training in drawing and modelling. Engravers such as Martin Schongauer and Albrecht Dürer were the sons of goldsmiths and Aldegrever was apprenticed to one.

Little books of patterns flooded from the printing presses in Nuremberg, Antwerp, Rome and Paris (but not London). Few survive in multiple copies. Albrecht Dürer, travelling through Italy and Flanders to expand his artistic experience, carried prints to give away and bought more on the way. The earliest example of Renaissance goldsmiths' work from London, the Howard Grace Cup (1525) takes its cast border of masks, urns and sheaves from a suite of designs by the German Hans Burgkmaier printed some 15 years earlier. It is clear that these sheets were circulating in London, since a writing desk made with the arms and initials of Henry VIII and Catherine of Aragon also incorporates motifs from Burgkmaier. In London and

Amsterdam at the end of the century designs for vases 'after the antique' published in Rome by Agostino da Veneziano (1528) were still being exploited, although they were mixed with more recently evolved Mannerist strapwork and marine subjects.

Although the colony of Italian artists gathered at Fontainebleau by Francis I (see 'Mannerism') is familiar to us from Benvenuto Cellini's description of his five years at Fontainebleau between 1540 and 1545, little French court plate survives. It continued to take the form of matching sets of ewers and basins, and decorated flagons for buffets characterized by great size and strong effects produced by striking combinations of such exotic materials as mother of pearl, alabaster or rock crystal.

Other European centres produced different styles. In Lisbon, the great wealth of the Portuguese crown, a result of its overseas discoveries in the fifteenth century, stimulated an extraordinary flowering of richly figurative chasing incorporating camels, palms and other African motifs rarely encountered in northern Europe. To set these inventive and intricately decorated dishes and basins beside the marine deities engraved by Androuet du Cerceau in about 1550, which were used by goldsmiths of Antwerp and Paris for basins in the following decade, is to recognize that the term 'Renaissance' retains little value when applied to goldsmiths' work of the mid-sixteenth century. A better distinction is between the earlier and later phases; the earlier 'antique' of before 1520, when architectural elements such as shell-niches, pilasters and busts in roundels were adopted as surface decoration on plate (as in the painting of interiors) and intermingled with the moresque and damask pattern drawn from Islamic metalwork.

The emergence around 1540 of Mannerist exaggeration, disseminated through the Antwerp engravers, rapidly swept away the delicate, well-proportioned shapes and horizontally layered ornament of the earlier phase. This fantastic style – great height and narrow feet, strapwork, elongated figures, monstrous forms for handles and spouts – was coarsely imitated and often misunderstood by goldsmiths supplying the market below court level. The style became standard in the later part of the sixteenth century, sustained and reinforced by its use in virtually all media, from tomb sculpture to tapestry. Strong traditions of exquisite control and technical supremacy, which extended to enamelling, distinguished the work of French- and particularly Paris-trained goldsmiths, as did the high silver content of their alloy. The 1995 exhibition in Paris of work by French Renaissance goldsmiths showed convincingly that, in comparison with English work of the same time, it had balance, proportion and delicacy of chasing, although a certain lack of invention.

The Burghley Nef, ostensibly a salt, is a Paris-made table fantasy in silvergilt and mother of pearl.

Spoons survive in far larger numbers than any other silver object from before 1700. Made and sold by silversmiths in every market town, spoons were given at baptism, passed on at death, offered as lottery prizes and required at election to corporations, colleges and livery companies. Although a silver spoon weighing one-and-a-half to two ounces was a luxury costing as much as an artisan earned in a week, these peculiarly personal objects were treasured by workmen, yeomen, widows and small shopkeepers. Very large numbers of spoons were accumulated by institutions through gift and purchase: more than 200 belonged to Eton College in 1456.

At a banquet each guest would expect the convenience of a spoon to dip into the communal dish. After a funeral feast of cakes and ale, and claret and wafers given for the mayor and citizens of Coventry in 1517, the Earl of Berkeley's steward was relieved to report to his master that none of his 20 dozen spoons had gone astray.

Until the 1660s the shape of spoons changed very little. The shallow fig-shaped bowl and faceted stem were hand-forged in one piece for strength and the decorative treatment was limited to the finial, which was separately modelled and cast.

The badge of the owner was often cast as the finial. The Earl of Rutland when ordering a set in 1542 paid extra for 'drawing' (designing) and fashioning his peacock crest. In 1581 the royal goldsmith Hugh Keal supplied seven dozen gilt spoons with Elizabeth I's device of 'pinickles' (pinnacles or pyramids) for the visit of French commissioners negotiating a marriage treaty.

Above: The fashionable Parisian women in Abraham Bosse's engraving are wielding their spoons and forks with aplomb, but table forks were still a matter for mockery in Jacobean London in 1616. The earliest known table fork (left) is from a set made for the marriage of John Manners, later Earl of Rutland, and Frances Montague in 1632. By the mid-1640s, when the children of Charles I were held in custody by Parliament, they were issued with personal sets of a knife, fork and spoon. Sucket forks for eating sticky desserts, such as green ginger, marchpane and preserved fruit, had been in use for more than 300 years.

Right: Sir Robert Tichborne, Lord Mayor of London in 1657, was presented with a set of gilt spoons made in London in 1592. The finials depict an unusual combination of images: the Nine Worthies, popular figures in medieval iconography, with Elizabeth I, Christ and St Peter. Only two complete sets of Tudor Apostle spoons survive. A set by Benjamin Yates at Goldsmiths' Hall (1626), uses six different casting models for the 12 figures.

Painted enamel was a technically difficult process and therefore costly. This delicate spoon, painted in a French or Flemish workshop, shows a monkey riding through the forest in a scene from a lost romance. It was intended to be treasured and admired rather than used. A cup from the same workshop and perhaps part of the same order is in the Metropolitan Museum of Art in New York.

Thomas Mangy, a goldsmith of York, made a set of death's head spoons for the Strickland family of Boynton in Yorkshire in about 1670. The skull and the inscription 'LIVE TO DIE' emphasize the vanity of human life. (Thomas Mangy came to a bad end; he was hanged for coin-clipping in 1696.) Death's head spoons were popular commemorative objects. In 1586 the Drapers' Company bought a set of 12 and had a feast in memory of their dead benefactor.

Medieval spoons. Left: Rouen-made spoon with a monster's head above the bowl. The town mark is struck in the bowl, a practice usual from the early 14th century. Centre: This spoon, with a wodewose (or wild man of the woods) finial, was probably made at Coggeshall in Essex. Right: Dug up near the river Wandle in Surrey, this spoon was made in London in 1493 and has a simple diamond point finial.

In this fashionable travelling set of gilded silver, made in London about 1690, the knife, fork and spoon unscrew to enable the owner to eat cleanly and with dignity away from his own table. A nutmeg grater, spice box and corkscrew are missing. Trefid or 'fork't' ends and flat handles, introduced from France at the Restoration, rapidly replaced the traditional English hexagonal handle. Because spoons and forks were laid in the French manner with bowls and prongs down on the tablecloth until the 1750s, armorials and engraving were concentrated on the reverse.

MANNERISM

In the middest a woman sytting uppon a dolphin, the handell of the eware being of crostike...standing uppon an antique head, the bodye of the eware chased with a band of antique with naked chyldren having whinges.

DESCRIPTION OF EWER AND BASIN
FROM THE PLATE INVENTORY OF THE FIRST EARL OF PEMBROKE, 1561

The distinction between Renaissance and Mannerist styles is not always easy to identify, since both were drawn from what was essentially the same vocabulary of Classical ornament. Invented in Italy as a court style in the 1530s, Mannerism both developed and rejected Renaissance conventions, reinterpreting and exaggerating the accepted formula. It rapidly spread through Europe, although it was not adopted everywhere in its most extreme forms. Conservative patrons and craftsmen continued to demand and make objects in an earlier manner well into the seventeenth century. And in some countries Mannerism was slow to make an impact but lasted longer. Like most stylistic conventions, its success depended on social, political and economic factors as well as purely artistic concerns. Much of our understanding of goldsmiths' work is dictated by the nature of surviving pieces and designs. Almost all of the most inventive French and Italian Mannerist silver, for example, has been lost or melted as a result of war, financial need and the changing demands of fashion.

The first major expression of Mannerism was the Palazzo del Te, designed and built for Duke Federico Gonzaga in Mantua by Giulio Romano from 1526. But the most comprehensive treatment was the decorative scheme for the palace of Fontainebleau in France, undertaken from 1530 by a team of Italian artists including Rosso Fiorentino and Francesco Primaticcio commissioned by Francis I. He also encouraged one of the supreme exponents of Mannerist goldsmiths' work, Benvenuto Cellini, to work at the French court.

Many of the trademarks of Mannerism made their first appearance at Fontainebleau and the style that came to permeate painting and architecture was rapidly applied to goldsmiths' work also. The horizontal layering and balanced use of ornament characteristic of the Renaissance was replaced by a stronger vertical emphasis with ornament of such complexity and concentration as often to be incomprehensible. Strapwork (the use of curled smooth bands reminiscent of leather straps), grotesque figures and masks, marine imagery, dolphins, nereids, sea monsters and shells were key elements. The natural world was a major source of inspiration, combined with a growing interest in the use of costly or exotic materials such as shells and hardstone. Exaggerated forms and impractical shapes became fashionable for plate. Ewers were set on unfeasible tiny feet, and handles made so sculptural as to be impossible to hold with comfort. Such objects were intended to be displayed rather than used, their exoticism reflecting the status of the patron. Central to the style was the concept of *dificultà*, implying complexity of design, virtuosity of execution and a challenge to the sophistication of the observer in unravelling what were often obscure philosophical, mythological or historical allusions. The ewer and basin from a set commissioned in 1621 is adorned with scenes specific to Grimaldi family history which relate to the decoration of their main residence in Genoa.

In this depiction of Solomon in the Temple from the Old Testament, the treasury is equipped with the most fashionable Mannerist plate, mainly secular in form.

The enormous influence of Fontainebleau was in part due to the speed with which the new designs and patterns were disseminated. Crucial to this process were prints, either engravings or woodcuts, which were widely available by the second half of the sixteenth century. The new style was seized upon in Antwerp in particular, a major economic centre, where not only was there a large number of goldsmiths (124 by 1557), but also several of the most influential designers, such as Erasmus Hornick, were active. Many prints were not intended specifically for goldsmiths. Genre scenes such as those in Jost Amman's *Kunstbuchlein* (1599) or the mid-century designs by Androuet du Cerceau and Etienne Delaune could be as well adapted for standing bowls in Limoges enamel as for silver. Ornament was further circulated through the sale and multiplication

throughout Europe of casting models and plaquettes in lead copied from wooden originals. From the 1560s Classical ornament began to be replaced by unified designs based on natural forms. Virgil Solis and the sculptor and architect Cornelius Floris, both based in Antwerp, were part of this movement. The latter was responsible for some extraordinary conceits, usually incorporating molluscs in some form.

Itinerant craftsmen were another important means of circulating new designs. Many goldsmiths travelled as part of their training, to develop expertise and widen their repertoire of designs. Courts acted as magnets for craftsmen, who assembled around major patrons in the cultural centres of Europe. One such focus was the Munich court of Duke Wilhelm V of Bavaria, and in Spain the redecoration of the Escorial undertaken by

This ewer and basin of 1621–2, with the arms of Giacomo Lomellini of Genoa, shows many of the exaggerated effects and rich detail typical of Mannerism.

Philip II brought an influx of Italian artists and craftsmen working in the Mannerist style. Spain's close political and economic links with Flanders also had an impact, but although Flemish designs did make their way there, Mannerism was not adopted with total enthusiasm. In Dresden Elector Augustus I of Saxony established another important workshop in the 1560s. Perhaps the most influential centre was Prague, where around 1600 the Holy Roman Emperor Rudolph II gathered some of the most talented goldsmiths of the day, such as Paul van Vianen and Christopher Jamnitzer (1563–1618) from Antwerp and Nuremberg respectively. From the middle of the century, a *Kunstkammer*, a collection of natural and man-made curiosities and precious

objects, was a fashionable necessity for any major patron. Mannerist goldsmiths' work, with its natural affinity with the bizarre and extraordinary, fitted with this concept originally devised in Medici Florence very well.

Wars and political upheavals also played a part in the movement of craftsmen. Religious persecution in the Netherlands in 1567 and 1569 and in France in 1572 forced Protestant goldsmiths to flee to sympathetic countries. Antwerp was similarly affected in the late sixteenth century. In England during Elizabeth I's reign there were probably as many as 500 active alien goldsmiths. There was also an influx of imported plate, often described as 'almain' or 'Norremberge' in inventories. This was in acknowledgement of the perceived superiority of German and Flemish silver and an indication of the determination of court patrons to acquire fashionable designs from abroad. The Earl of Pembroke's ewer and basin may have been imported or made in England in the new style; it seems likely that the more skilful pieces were either made by alien craftsmen or followed imported designs. In any case, both objects and craftsmen created great difficulties for the Goldsmiths' Company, since the alloy used was not as pure as English sterling silver, and so could not be hallmarked, and English goldsmiths were hostile to foreigners.

An important source of work for Mannerist goldsmiths was southern Germany, thanks to a silver industry established in the previous century and based in Nuremberg and Augsburg. The economic wealth of both cities, their close trade links with Antwerp and the growing significance as patrons of the wealthy merchant classes and the guilds all provided an atmosphere in which goldsmiths could flourish. The guilds and civic institutions in particular had specific needs for presentation and display plate, such as the grand standing cups that were offered to visiting dignitaries. This was often not in the forefront of fashion but drew on Mannerist ornament. Strapwork rapidly became ubiquitous and grotesques were added to stems or finials. Ordinary table plate such as beakers and tankards paid lip-service to Mannerism while avoiding its wilder excesses. This extensive yet conservative output coexisted with some of the most sophisticated and elaborate Mannerist creations, made for the most discerning patrons in Europe. One of the most important workshops of the period was that of Wenzel Jamnitzer (1508–85) in Nuremberg. He worked for four Holy Roman Emperors and produced some of the most outstanding Mannerist designs, including the famous Merckel tablecentre of 1549 now in the Rijksmuseum, Amsterdam. Jamnitzer was renowned for pioneering new techniques, such as casting from life the small plants, insects and shellfish that often featured in Mannerist design.

By the early years of the seventeenth century, Mannerism was in decline throughout Europe. Italy was already looking towards the Baroque, and in Nuremberg the search for an alternative was manifested by what was in effect a Gothic revival, led by the workshop of Hans Petzold and drawing inspiration from Albrecht Dürer's lobed designs of a century before. The Low Countries were moving in yet another direction as a result of the designs emerging from the Utrecht workshops of the brothers Paul and Adam van Vianen. The auricular style, drawn from the fantastic mollusc-based designs of Cornelius Floris, stands apart from Mannerism with its fleshy, dissolving grotesquerie based on marine imagery. It had considerable impact in England through Adam van Vianen's son Christian who was invited to court and offered a pension in 1630 by Charles I. With its bizarre dynamics, unity of design and inherent theatricality, the auricular stands on the cusp between Mannerism and Baroque.

The monstrous and the marine are much in evidence in this engaging design for a ewer by Cornelius Floris, which was probably never executed.

Charles I took a keen interest in goldsmiths' work, collecting outstanding works of art in silver as well as bronzes and painting, and introduced a distinctive new style to English court plate. His taste was for the fleshy, sensuous silver of the van Vianen family and their Flemish contemporaries. Unfortunately almost nothing survives from his private collection and very little of the plate ordered from the Jewel House during his reign.

The accumulation and display of 'curiously wrought' examples of goldsmiths' work was a princely tradition. The Danish royal collection at Rosenborg Castle in Copenhagen and those of the Wittelsbach family in the

Charles I dined in public, often with Henrietta Maria, two or three times a week. Although the setting here is not an exact representation of the Queen's apartments in Whitehall Palace, the spectators, the formality, the covered gilt dishes and the absence of glasses on the table all agree with contemporary descriptions.

These boxes containing sets of 36 counters cast with the heads of Charles I and Henrietta Maria were used for gambling or checking arithmetic. Such small popular commemorative items were made in large numbers and rarely marked. More costly accessories, such as gold tobacco boxes, carried the King's image too.

Residenzmuseum at Munich are rare survivors of this court practice. Charles inherited a keen eye for artistic achievement in silver from his mother, Anne of Denmark, who owned silver furniture, including firedogs with cupids as finials. Charles built up a collection of silver plaques chased with scenes from Ovid's *Metamorphoses* for his private collection at Whitehall Palace and commissioned display plate from Antwerp, still a leading artistic centre. He also encouraged foreign craftsmen to settle in London, principally Christian van Vianen from the famous family of Utrecht silversmiths. Van Vianen's workshop in Westminster, which was staffed by Dutch workmen who specialized in complex high-relief figurative chasing, was effectively beyond the control of the Goldsmiths' Company. As well as supplying the King himself with such pieces as the elaborate and costly altar set for the Order of the Garter (stolen in 1642), it also made plate for the English aristocracy.

Charles I's personal silver was pawned, melted, stolen or otherwise dispersed during the Civil War and the remaining Jewel House plate was sold with the rest of the royal possessions between 1649 and 1650. Ironically, the largest group of Stuart royal silver to survive is the gilt buffet plate that Charles sold to the Tsar of Russia in 1626 and 1627. These large display pieces, including antiquarian copies of Henry VIII's water pots made for James I, are on show today in the Kremlin Armouries, Moscow.

This tall covered cup chased with the Stuart royal badges was made in 1626 for Thomas Coventry, Keeper of the Great Seal to James I. In accordance with custom, on the king's death he was given the discarded seal matrices (120 ounces of silver) to make this cup, weighing almost the same (123 ounces).

Figurative modelling and chasing were highly esteemed. Peter-Paul Rubens designed this rosewater basin with the birth of Venus and marine imagery of crabs, coral and shells. The basin, with a ewer, was made in Antwerp, Rubens's home town, by Theodore Rogiers. They vanished from the royal collection, probably during the Civil War.

This basin was raised from a single sheet of silver. Two writhing dolphins enclose a pool of water, gushing from a grotesque mask where their heads meet. This illusionistic effect is typical of the silver of the van Vianen family of Utrecht. Christian van Vianen who signed the basin in 1632 came to London in that year to work for Charles I.

The scene shows a banquet held to celebrate the official opening in 1593 of the Schloss Kirchensittenbach in Germany. The city architect is offering the tall green welcome cup, probably ceramic or glass in this instance, to the guests.

On the table are a number of pieces of ceremonial silver, including a double standing cup and two grand covered beakers. A flagon and wine bottle are cooling in the cistern on the floor.

Ceremonies involving drinking and the formal exchange of gifts on arrival and departure were occasions of great significance in Europe. Since the medieval period specific types of silver vessel were developed for such rituals, the form varying according to local practice. In Germany the *Wilkomm* or welcome cup was offered to arriving guests at formal dinners and banquets, such as those held by guilds, brotherhoods or societies, or to commemorate a special occasion. Welcome cups were generally tall, on a long stem, covered and as elaborate and costly as possible, since their grandeur reflected the status of the host. They were also popular in the form of animals with removable heads. In 1607 the Venetian envoy to Zurich described in a letter to the Doge how he had attended a city banquet, and presented the councillors with a vessel in the shape of a gilded silver lion 'after which they followed the custom of their country according to which they handed round the lion and each drank in turn, more than once and in increasing high spirits'. He added that 'they highly prize these gifts and display them like the treasures of a church'.

This tazza, or standing bowl, was made in Zurich around 1675. It is one of the few surviving examples of a bath cup, identified by the inscription around the rim which states that it was given as such to the Stadthalter, or city governor. The subject of the engraving inside the bowl – Joseph feasting his brethren – is not directly relevant to bathing, although the inscription draws a parallel between giving a feast and a bath gift.

A similar custom developed in spa towns, in particular Baden, famous for its waters since the Roman period. Here visitors would offer a gift, often a silvergilt cup, to the city officials on arrival and receive one in return. The design by Johann Theodor de Bry (about 1600) for a tazza bowl representing a Roman bath would have been an appropriate subject.

This cup of 1717 is identified by an inscription as the *Wilkomm* of the Hanover Grünehagener Brotherhood. This primarily financial association, founded in 1616, provided free funerals for its members and their families. Unsurprisingly, new members had to be under 40, in good health and of 'blameless character'. Paupers and soldiers were excluded. The inscriptions on the cup and pendant shields all refer in some way to death.

This is the lower part of a gilt double standing cup made in southern Germany in about 1590. Such cups were frequently used as welcome cups, since they were composed of two identical halves and made two goblets when separated. When assembled, it would have been displayed with other grand plate on a buffet. A similar example can be seen on the table in the dining scene opposite.

This German design of around 1600 is for a wager cup, which was constructed in such a way that it could not be set down until it had been drained and upturned. It would have been passed from hand to hand around the table. Cups in the form of a grandly dressed woman were often used at weddings.

The high relief of the battle scene on this Jacob Bodendick tankard of around 1670 illustrates the skill of alien craftsmen.

BAROQUE

The term 'Baroque', like 'Gothic', was coined in the eighteenth century as a pejorative epithet. It probably derived from the Spanish or Portuguese word for a deformed pearl, and Baroque design was seen as an equally grotesque mockery of natural forms, in defiance of aesthetics and sense. Its modern meaning is more positive: it is an architectural style. When architectural forms and principles were applied to silver the results were theatrical, grand, three-dimensional and often boldly sculptural. The vocabulary was Classical, as was that of Mannerism, but the Baroque style was a reaction against the convoluted imagery and microscopic delicacy of Mannerism. Architectural features such as volutes, friezes, 's' scrolls, caryatid figures, putti and acanthus were central to it. Panels of finely embossed or chased scenes were integrated into designs just as painting and sculpture were melded into architectural interiors. This unity of design did not apply only to objects, but also to buildings and their interiors. The architect–designer who oversaw every element, such as Charles le Brun, was pivotal to this process.

The dissemination of the style gained a powerful impetus, particularly in Italy, as the language of Roman Catholicism after the Counter-Reformation. In practical terms, Church treasuries had to be re-equipped with impressive liturgical silver. The Baroque period also saw dramatic developments across Europe in serving, eating and table etiquette, the appearance of new foods and drinks and the growing sophistication of domestic rituals generally. These required a range of new silver tableware and furnishings, which triggered new designs and an vast increase in demand for silver.

In contrast to the growth in production, the seventeenth century was also a period of political unrest across Europe, with consequent losses of silver plate.

The Baroque style was emerging in Rome as early as the 1590s but it was not until the second quarter of the seventeenth century that it appeared in silver, disseminated through engravings. Rome continued to be an important source of inspiration for European goldsmiths, partly because of the presence of Gian Lorenzo Bernini and architects such as Francesco Borromini, but also because major patrons – the papacy, the Church, the aristocracy and civic institutions – were commissioning large amounts of ecclesiastical and other plate. Little of this survives, but that which remains, such as the papal mace made by Giovanni da Forli, often manifests the bold sculptural qualities of the best Baroque design.

As a result of the inspired patronage of Louis XIV, whose personal rule began in 1661, it was to France that the discerning looked for fashionable developments. The court style was in effect an extension of Italian Baroque, and several of the key practitioners, such as le Brun and Jean le Pautre, visited Italy to acquaint themselves with the source. As their designs began to circulate through Europe, the French interpretation of Baroque spread. Travelling goldsmiths helped this process. Le Pautre's own etchings were copied by the Swiss journeyman Dietrich Meyer, whose sketchbook records his travels between 1669 and 1674 from Switzerland to Augsburg and the Netherlands.

It was through Louis' grand architectural programmes, principally that undertaken at Versailles from 1669, that the French court style gained its coherence. The royal manufactory was established at Gobelins in 1667 to provide fittings and furniture for the sumptuous interiors conceived as an integrated whole, and many of the most illustrious Parisian goldsmiths, Nicholas Delaunay and Claude Ballin I among them, were employed to produce literally tons of spectacular plate. Little of this output survived for long, since Louis' expensive and incessant military campaigns led to wholesale surrenders of silver to the Mint in 1689 and 1709.

The most extravagant items produced for the French court were silver furniture, status symbols *par excellence*, such as grand ensembles of mirrors, standing candlesticks and tables. This taste rapidly spread to the Netherlands and England during the reign of Charles II, and to those among the aristocracy who could afford such luxuries. John Evelyn described the 'great vases of wrought plate, tables, stands, chimney furniture, sconces, branches' owned by the Duchess of Portland in 1683. Most surviving silver furniture was made in Augsburg, by this period the most important goldsmithing centre in Germany, and exported as widely as Denmark, Sweden and Russia. By 1696 Augsburg had 204 goldsmiths producing and exporting vast quantities of display plate of all types.

Augsburg was also one of the major sources of tableware, which ranged from simple beakers and tankards to the equipment needed for the revolution in table manners and etiquette that emanated from the French court during the second half of the seventeenth century. It became fashionable to furnish rooms specially for the purpose of dining and to provide each diner with individual dishes and cutlery, rather than to rely on communal bowls. Serving dishes began to be set on the table, rather than placed on a buffet to the side. Footed salvers, for offering food and drink, appeared. This increasingly sophisticated approach fuelled the demand for plate in sets with matching ornament – the beginnings of the modern dinner service. At the same time, new drinks were introduced into the social canon. In England in the 1680s the taste for punch and red wine led to the invention of the monteith with its notched sides for suspending and cooling glasses. Perhaps most important was the growing trend through the second half of the century for the new hot drinks – tea, coffee and chocolate.

Revolutions were also occurring elsewhere in domestic etiquette. Foremost was the emergence of the toilet service, a collection of matching implements and containers for display and use while dressing. The larger assemblies, which ran to 30 or more pieces, also included eating and writing equipment. The concept of the toilette, as it originated in France, often encompassed a private meal. Toilet services were often given as wedding gifts. They were a response to the growing elaboration of social ritual within the home, and, in the courtly sense, of the reinforcement of status and they afforded considerable opportunities for the goldsmith. Again, Augsburg was in the forefront of production of these luxurious sets, although important examples were also made in the Hague, Paris and London.

England was very much under the political and cultural influence of France after the Restoration of 1660 when Charles II returned from exile with a well-developed French taste. In the 1690s Daniel Marot, who probably designed for the French court, worked for William of Orange first in the Netherlands and then in England. His many published designs for objects ranging from silver and ironwork to upholstery and chimneypieces were enormously influential in popularizing French design. The assimilation of French taste was accelerated following the Revocation of the

This papal mace, made by a Roman goldsmith about 1700, is a physical expression of the princely ceremony of the Church.

Edict of Nantes in 1685 which drove Protestant crafts-men out of France, many of them to England. The Huguenots had a dramatic impact on English silver, not only because of the high standard of craftsmanship and so the competition they posed to the indigenous craft, but also because of their knowledge of French designs demanded by fashionable patrons. By the turn of the century, the French style was dominant and the Huguenots themselves well established, to the dismay of the English workmen. Helmet-shaped ewers and cut-card work are two examples of the new forms and decorative techniques. In addition to producing high-quality work, the French-trained goldsmiths cut costs by adopting casting techniques unfamiliar in England. The influx came not only from France. Netherlandish goldsmiths, Christian van Vianen, Jean-Gerard Cocques and Jacob Bodendick among them, were invited to work for the court of Charles II, establishing large workshops employing alien craftsmen. The Dutch connection was further strengthened after the accession of William III in 1688.

During the late seventeenth and early eighteenth centuries, high Baroque began to give way to increas-ingly diverse styles. One of these was chinoiserie, a reinterpretation of oriental motifs and forms inspired by porcelain and lacquerwork. This became briefly popular in England and the Netherlands in the 1680s as a result of closer trading links with China and a series of engrav-ings of the Dutch embassy to Peking published in 1669. In France from the 1670s there were signs that an alter-native to the massively architectural qualities of Italian Baroque was being sought. This was exemplified in the work of Jean Berain, who produced designs for silver in a light, two-dimensional manner, ornamented with flat patterns drawing on a Mannerist vocabulary of grotesques, cartouches and delicate scrolled bands. The dainty effect thus created rapidly spread through Europe, partly by means of prints. It was seized upon by Augsburg goldsmiths such as Gottlieb Menzel and Johann Erhard II Heuglin and applied particularly to toilet services. This so-called 'Régence' style provided the seedbed for the Rococo.

The political symbolism of the cock, chained lion and eagle suggest that
this frame may have been made to hold a portrait of Louis XIV.

From the mid-17th century tea, coffee and chocolate entered Europe from China, Arabia and Central America. Drunk hot, these drinks appeared startlingly novel to a population who had previously quenched their thirst on cold small beer and hot possets. In a letter to Lord Tweeddale in 1743, Duncan Forbes wrote: 'Tea...is now become so common that the meanest familys, even of labouring people...make their morning's meal of it, and thereby wholly disuse the ale, which heretofore was their accustomed drink.'

The methods of preparation, the equipment and the accompanying rituals wrought great social change. Coffee, imported through Turkish merchants, brought with it the Arabian coffee house. By 1675 London had over 250 coffee houses, which also sold chocolate and alcohol. Almost exclusively a male

This early 18th-century Dutch coffee urn has the three legs and tap typical of continental coffeewares. It stood over a burner to keep the contents hot. The pear-shaped model later adopted all over Europe was itself superseded by the vase shape of the late 18th century. Coffee was drunk with sugar and milk from its first arrival in Europe.

This early chocolate cup and stand from a set of six made in the early 1690s is gilded and elaborately decorated. Pairs of chocolate cups often accompanied toilet services and their design and costly finish reflect the high status of this delicacy. De Quelus recommended sucking a block and washing it down: 'the wheels and springs of our machine [are] mended, health is preserved, and life prolonged.'

As in the van Aken painting, this Rococo tea kettle and stand would have stood away from the tea-table to avoid accidents. A continuous supply of hot water was necessary to replenish small teapots. From the late 17th century advice on the correct way to drink black tea advocated the addition of milk and/or sugar. The use of sugar hastened the universal popularity of hot drinks in Europe.

English imports of tea outstripped those of coffee and chocolate. In 1734 Twinings sold 13,114 lb of tea, 5,137 lb of coffee and 2,897 lb of chocolate. Until 1786 tea was heavily taxed and black tea at 14s. a pound cost a craftsman a week's wages. The drink created a new social ceremony for women, and was a popular subject for 18th-century paintings, as illustrated here in *The Tea Party* by Van Aken of about 1720.

domain, they attracted tradesmen, intellectuals and writers. Lloyd's coffee house in London developed into the world's largest insurance company. As coffee became fashionable, women began to drink it in their own apartments.

Early 18th-century English inventories show that coffee utensils were outnumbered two to one by tea wares. In 1685 the East India Committee noted that it was the 'Thea...which will colour the water in which it is infused, most of a greenish complexion is generally best accepted', but by the 1720s the cheaper black tea had become more popular. Green tea (Bing or Imperial, Heyson and Singlo) was unfermented and needed time to brew; black or fermented tea (Pekoe, Souchon, Congo and Bohea) tasted better with milk and sugar.

Chocolate was introduced from Mexico by the Spaniards in the early 16th century. It never achieved the popularity of tea or coffee, perhaps because until the 19th century it was troublesome to prepare and serve. Early chocolate was flavoured with sugar and spices to improve the taste and drunk scalding hot between cooling draughts of water. The fashion plate illustrates a pot of chocolate being stirred.

This small teapot for green tea is similar to the one in the van Aken painting. The wooden handle protected the pourer from the great heat of the metal. Silver was found to be unsuitable for tea bowls and cups.

THE ARRIVAL OF THE DINNER SERVICE

An Englishman's table is remarkably clean, the linen is very white, the plate shines brightly, and knives and forks are changed surprisingly often...everytime a plate is removed. When everybody has done eating, the table is cleared, the cloth even being removed, and a bottle of wine with a glass for each guest is placed on the table.

CHARLES DE SAUSSURE, 1726

After about 1700 the new emphasis in the dining room shifted attention from the sideboard display to the table. The traditional buffet was set out with gilt plate, of which much, such as ewers and basins or flagons, was now redundant although still an index of standing, wealth and descent. The Goldsmiths' Company commissioned John Linnell to design a 'Beaufet' so they could display the magnificent Rococo plate they were ordering from Paul de Lamerie.

In *service à la française* the first course or 'remove' was already placed on the table when diners were seated and they subsequently served themselves from the choice of dishes within reach. Servants performed only the most basic duties during the meal: passing round oil, vinegar and bread, and bringing glasses and drink from the sideboard as called for.

The dinner service incorporated variously shaped dishes, rather than simple round platters, which after the early 1730s were increasingly decorated to a common theme. Engravings of recommended table layouts can be seen in *The Modern Cook* (2nd edn, 1736) by Vincent La Chapelle, cook to Lord Chesterfield. Condiments were often assembled around an epergne, an ornate visual centrepiece for the new highly integrated table layout. The epergne originated in the

1690s at the French court (where it was known as the *surtout*) when Louis XIV's goldsmiths evolved a silver centrepiece for the King. A large tureen stood in the centre, surrounded by cruets and casters that could be replaced with candle stands and dishes for sweetmeats at a later stage of the meal. The earliest epergnes with English hallmarks, dating from 1730, closely resemble the French models recorded in designs collected for the Swedish court by Nicodemus Tessin. The English adopted the French word *epergne* which means 'treasury', as in 'the pleasures of the table brought together', or 'sparing', for without the constant interruption of servants a sitting could be more intimate. Like virtually all French silver of Louis' reign, the first epergne has vanished, thanks to his incessant wars and sumptuary laws. Also very little of the work made by the master-craftsmen patronized by Louis XV and XVI – Claude Ballin, François-Thomas Germain, Jacques Roettiers and Robert-Joseph Auguste – survived the Revolution.

The centrepiece became a vehicle for fanciful design in the 1740s and '50s. The two made for Frederick Louis, Prince of Wales, one to a pergola design by William Kent and the other, the *Poseidon*, by Nicholas Sprimont, had their accompanying condiments and sauceboats in the same themes, and are still in the Royal Collection, although altered in the nineteenth century. Another, more extravagant still and the peak of Augsburg design and craft skill, is the centrepiece on a musical and hunting theme made for the Prince-Bishop of Hildesheim in 1761–63.

Soup, served in a highly decorated round tureen, opened the meal. The tureen, or *pot à l'oille*, was

The Chesterfield wine cooler, London, 1727–78, mark of Paul Crespin (1694–1770)
overstriking that of Paul de Lamerie (1688–1751).

another vessel that evolved at the French court. Marine subjects, game and vegetable motifs may have indicated the contents, or more likely were admired as challenging the goldsmiths' skill in imitating nature. Juste-Aurèle Meissonier's *Livre des legumes*, published in 1734 and re-issued in England in 1757, contains the inspiration for the cauliflowers, artichokes and turnips that appear on tureens from the 1730s to the 1760s. The new culinary trend for soups, stews and 'made dishes' with sauces rather than roasts, also brought a demand for specialized silver serving spoons, for soup, ragout and veal or beef olives.

The new dinner services were at first the preserve of the monarchy and the highest nobility, who might be able to obtain this costly necessity from the Jewel House through royal office or subsidize payment with their old plate. However, as the goldsmiths increasingly standardized shape and ornament, minor nobility, gentry, professionals and clerics could emulate the aristocracy by acquiring a service over time as funds allowed.

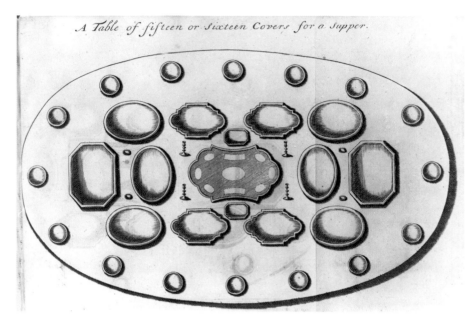

Engraving of table layout, from Vincent La Chapelle's *The Modern Cook*, 1736.

Although made in different workshops and at different times, the service was unified by common motifs.

The fashion for complete dinner services after the French model had a relatively short life. Although silver, commonly engraved with the owner's armorials, was a well-established status symbol and a safe investment, Chinese porcelain factories began making armorial services to order from the 1720s. Then, from the mid-century, porcelain from Meissen and the English factories at Chelsea, Bow, Worcester and Derby challenged silver's supremacy. This was especially true for confectionery and dessert dishes, for which, in the words of Thomas Pownall MP in 1769, 'nothing of metal...would be conformable to ye present whim of Tast'.

The service of wine was an elaborate and ceremonious procedure, demanding silver items in many forms, from the massive cooler to the tiny bottle-ticket. Wine was poured into glasses at the sideboard and brought to the table on salvers. Popular too were various mixed drinks, often brandy-based, which were prepared by gentlemen for themselves at the table or at race meetings. These were served from punch bowls with ladles and strainers. Until the late seventeenth century, wine was still brought up from barrels in the cellar in dark onion-shaped glass bottles or in silver decanter jugs. After the re-discovery of the bottle-cork in the mid-seventeenth century, it was realized that wine improved with ageing in the bottle. By the end of the eighteenth century the bottle had evolved into the straighter, more cylindrical form familiar today, which is easier both to cork and store. A more elegant solution to bringing wine to the table was sought and the clear lead glass decanter, first made by Ravenscroft in the 1680s, became common by 1750.

By 1720 silver bottle-tickets arrived and replaced parchment labels. Since bottle tickets did not legally have to be sent for assay until 1790, earlier examples can only be dated when the maker sent them voluntarily. The early labels were nearly all escutcheon- or shield-shaped, echoing the design of handles on contemporary furniture. Benjamin Mildmay paid 5s. 6d. each for fourteen tickets in 1738, and George Booth, second Earl of Warrington, had a set of ten in 1750, including tickets for champagne, methuen (a Portuguese wine), red and white port, mild ale and strong beer, weighing between 14 and 16 pennyweight each.

The bottle slide or plate, as the wine coaster was originally known, was devised about 1720 to save the table from scratches. Brought in after the main meal and dessert were finished, when the table had been cleared of dishes and coverings and the women dismissed to drink tea, the men could pass the wine to each other in a more relaxed atmosphere.

On the sideboards of the grandest houses stood a cistern and fountain, with a cooler beneath. Normally designed as a set and often ornamented with the heraldic supporters of the owner, they were by far the largest and most impressive objects connected with the serving of wine. Water from the fountain washed the glasses in the cistern, and the cooler, which was filled with iced water, chilled the wine between servings. A cooler made in 1701 by Philip Rollos for George Booth, with its heraldic demi-boars for handles, weighs 1,100 ounces and holds over 20 gallons.

By the second half of the century the smaller table-top cooler, or 'ice-paile', for a single bottle was more common. Originally a French refinement, an early English reference appears in the 1701 Jewel House

issue of ambassadorial plate to the Earl of Marlborough in Holland. As with other silver for serving wine, these pieces were highly decorated and costly. A pair made for the Earl of Chesterfield by Paul de Lamerie and Paul Crespin cost about ten shillings an ounce, within the top range of prices for such excellent workmanship.

The eighteenth century saw the evolution of a number of smaller silver gadgets, such as tasters and funnels, to accompany the rituals of wine drinking, still considered in the wine trade the ideal medium for tasting and assessing the colour of wine. Corkscrews, first recorded in 1681 as 'steele wormes', often had a silver handle. Kept in the pocket, these were short and delicate objects designed to extract the tapered corks of the early bottles. Another silver item often to be found in a man's pocket was a nutmeg grater for preparing spiced wine, punch or other mixed drinks. Elaborate strainers for lemon and orange juice, also made of silver, were decoratively pierced.

Drawing of Louis XIV's personal tureen designed by Nicolas-Ambroise Cousinet for the Swedish court, about 1690.

The table was the centre of social activity in the 17th and 18th centuries and, as earlier in polite society, the silver with which it was dressed reflected the wealth and social standing of the host. Ambassadors going overseas to represent the English crown were given an allowance of several thousand ounces of silver and silvergilt plate by the Jewel House. Most chose elaborate silver tableware, expensively decorated in the latest fashion. Tureens, ladles and epergnes on the table and wine coolers and salvers on the buffet were a calculated and conspicuous display of English wealth and power.

Books of etiquette, generally written by cooks to the nobility, dictated behaviour at table and contained recipes, diagrams and instruction on how certain dishes should be carved, served and laid out. In *The Complete Practical Cook* (1730), Charles Carter, cook to the Duke of Argyll, published 60 table layouts for

various occasions. The most elaborate was the Coronation Dinner for George II at Westminster Hall for which three tables of 46 settings are detailed on foldout pages. Plate was hired or borrowed for such grand dinners.

These manuals of correctness even extended to the behaviour of the servants attending at table. In 1788 John Trusler recommended 'give nothing but on a waiter' (a small tray) and that the left hand should be used when serving wine, with the thumb placed on the foot of the glass to prevent it toppling over. This advice is enacted by the servant to the left of the painting by Pieter Angellis.

This painting is rich in information. The search for silver leads our eye into the depths of the cupboard to the right of the scene. There, drawn to our attention by the open arms of one of the servants, is the silver, displayed on the bare shelves in the manner of a buffet. It is a fine illustration of the types of object in common use in the early 18th-century dining room. Sets of plain silver plates for the first course sit unceremoniously stacked, while the larger meat and serving dishes stand to attention behind.

On the second shelf stands an early cruet frame for oil and vinegar. This type developed into the larger and more sophisticated Warwick frame in which glass cruets and the traditional set of three casters for mustard, pepper and sugar sit together. Sets of casters were customary from the 1660s. The plain body of a caster offered a generous surface that could be exploited for the owner's heraldry, an essential decorative feature of dining plate.

Matching services of silver flatware in two sizes, for the main course and the dessert, became standard and were housed in decorative boxes on the sideboard. The spoons are missing from this knife box of about 1765.

Left: As a result of the 18th-century preoccupation with elegant dining, distinctive types of serving equipment were developed. This broad-bladed fish server with intricate floral piercing has been cast and engraved, and is a standard type of server with the mark of Thomas Nash (1770).

Below: Elaborate sauceboats and tureens of silver have become associated with the flamboyant excesses of Rococo design and the practicalities of the metal forgotten. Silver is hygienic, sterile and, when pre-warmed, vessels for food and sauces retain heat well. This was important when the 'first remove' dishes had to be brought from a distant kitchen and set out on the table before the diners sat down.

Left: The silver scallop shell (London, 1749–50) is a surprisingly early example of kitchen-to-tableware. A recipe of 1723 gives instructions on its use: 'Lay a piece of Sweet Butter at the Bottom of your Silver Scallop Shell; then get a quantity of Large Oysters, and cut off the fins; put four in a shell, with some of their own liquor strain'd, grated Bread, a little Salt, Pepper, and a spoonful of white wine, and cover them with grated Bread, and set them over your stove to stew; and hold over them your Browning-Iron; half an hour will stew them.'

REDISCOVERY OF THE ANTIQUE

To Mr Adam's taste in the ornament of his buildings and furniture we stand indebted, in as much as manufacturers of every kind felt, as it were, the electric power of this revolution in Art.

SIR JOHN SOANE, 1812

The architect Robert Adam (1728–92), whose name has become synonymous with a particularly English interpretation of the Neo-Classical style, returned from Italy to set up his London practice in 1758. Over the next 10 years, as Adam's commissions and influence grew, a complete alteration in taste was occurring throughout Europe. The frivolity and excess of the Rococo gave way to the symmetry and order of what contemporaries called the 'true' or 'correct' style. The Classical revival was not simply a reaction; the Classical past had never been out of fashion and the Grand Tour had to include visits to Paris and Rome. While it was undoubtedly an age of intellectual excitement during which universal truths were sought amongst the Classical models, there may have been more pragmatic reasons for seeking inspiration in Greek and Roman art. The burgeoning industries trumpeted their improvements to modern manufacture through a return to familiar Classical shapes and ornament as a way of reassuring consumers faced with a huge choice of new products. Every branch of art and manufactures was affected from ceramics, where Sèvres and Wedgwood led the field, to the silver of the Parisian, London, Sheffield and Birmingham workshops.

Excavations at Herculaneum (begun 1738) and Pompeii (begun 1755) were extending the understanding of the Classical world. These sites gave unprecedented access to the decoration of domestic

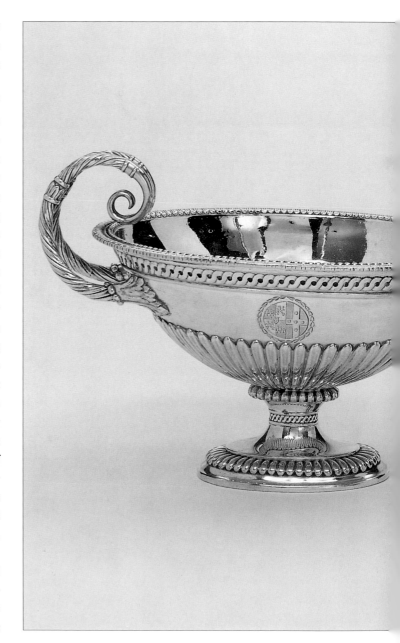

interiors and provided fresh inspiration for designers hungry for new motifs. Information about these and other Classical remains was disseminated through personal experience as well as a flood of publications. Architects such as Adam and his contemporary Sir William Chambers (1732–96) studied in Italy. Adam, influenced by the artists Giovanni Piranesi and Charles-Louis Clerisseau, visited and drew many of the important archaeological sites. He returned to England with a portfolio that contained a rich repertoire of forms and ornament. In addition he brought with him old master paintings to sell in London. He was not alone in importing art and antiques: connoisseurs such as Sir William Hamilton introduced Classical art to a wider public. Not only did part of his collection of Greek vases become the property of the nation in 1772

Pair of sauceboats designed by Robert Adam for Sir Watkin Williams-Wynn, 1773–74.

but from 1766 they were published in four volumes (*Catalogue of Etruscan, Greek and Roman Antiquities*) by the French art historian d'Hancarville.

This was one of many publications that gave those who could not travel access to Classical models. The most important works for silver designers and manufacturers were the architectural studies of Robert Wood and James Dawkins *The Ruins of Palmyra* (1753), Comte de Caylus's *Receuil d'antiquités* (1752–67), and James Stuart and Nicholas Revett's *Antiquities of Athens* (1762–88). Many of these works had a didactic purpose. D'Hancarville introduced his volumes with the hope that 'we make an agreeable present to our Manufacturers of earthenware and China, and to those who make vases in silver, copper, glass, marble etc... being besides in great want of models, they will find here more than two hundred forms, the greatest part of which are absolutely new to them; then, as in a plentiful stream, they may draw ideas which their ability and taste will know how to improve to their advantage, and to that of the public.'

In contrast to the elaborate and often ponderous *gout grec* fashionable in France from the early 1760s and adapted by Sir William Chambers for his aristocratic clients, the Neo-Classical style popularized by Adam was a more elegant and spirited affair. As d'Hancarville suggests, silversmiths and their patrons were free to choose from the growing selection of form and ornament. Some silver was more archaeologically correct in detail than others but since none owed a debt to Graeco-Roman plate complete imitation was not an issue. It was not until the nineteenth century that Roman silver was recovered in any quantity. Inspiration came from other materials such as marble and ceramics. Some shapes, for example the urn, could be adapted to numerous functions in silver from tea caddies and tureens to racing cups. Candlesticks had drawn upon the Classical column since the 1660s but now looked to a wider repertoire of ornament. Teapots, bread baskets and wine coolers required more ingenuity, but by adapting shape and decoration manufacturers were able to create a harmonious and symmetrically balanced object.

Large areas of silver were left plain and in the best examples the restrained ornament complemented the elegance of the form. The most frequent decorations were cast and applied or chased floral swags, ram's heads, palmettes, acanthus leaves with the occasional use of Classical medallions. Less costly plate attempted to convey only a plausible semblance of Neo-Classical style in which archaeological correctness had no place. Bright-cut engraving, piercing and fluted decoration were more important to makers of this kind of silver. Adam was commissioned by wealthy clients such as Sir Watkin Williams-Wynn to design plate as part of decorative interior schemes. His influence on silver design was due in part to his architectural work and publications although some of his silver was undoubtedly inspirational. The Richmond Cup race prize made by Daniel Smith and Robert Sharp in 1770 became a model for silversmiths. Several other architects designed for silver, including Chambers and James Wyatt (1748–1813) who provided the manufacturer Matthew Boulton with designs.

The leading exponent of the regional silversmiths, Matthew Boulton (1728–1809) was a cultured man who moved in the most avant-garde scientific and artistic circles of his day. He was both an entrepreneur and an innovator who produced some high-quality silver but he is remembered for his collaboration with James Watt which produced the steam engine. The extension of the assay to allow silver to be marked in Birmingham was another of his successes. Boulton took an important part in the rapid growth of technical experiments which stimulated industrial production. Increasingly, standardized goods were made at a price that more and more consumers could afford. Until the late eighteenth century London had been the premier centre in England for the making of silver. This pre-eminence, particularly at the lower end of the market, was challenged by the quantity and, in some cases, the quality of silver from factories such as Soho, Boulton's showcase outside Birmingham built in 1762. He capitalized on the new techniques of manufacture and decoration pioneered by the Sheffield plate manufacturers (see 'Imitations and Substitutes').

View of Matthew Boulton's factory at Soho, Birmingham, 1781.

The rolling mill, which produced sheets of metal of a uniform thickness, had been in use since about 1740 but more recent developments had included the fly press, which permitted accurate and repetitive piercing, and improvements to the metal alloys to improve the accuracy and complexity of die-stamping. More decorative components could now be made by this process. The candlesticks for which Sheffield became well known could be made entirely from such stamped elements and a great variety of models achieved by interchanging the decorative parts. Boulton, who began making silver in about 1766, used these modern industrial techniques where appropriate for both silver and Sheffield plate but did not entirely replace traditional craft skills with mechanization. The advantages for the customer of machine-made goods were obvious. Candlesticks at Soho could be made from stampings at a price substantially lower than by casting in London. One pattern, the 'Lyon' candlestick, sold for £17. 2s. compared to £44. 11s; the stamped candlesticks required only 38 ounces of silver as opposed to 108 ounces needed for casting.

Consumers could economize further by buying Sheffield plate rather than silver. Plated wares were sold side by side in London shops from 1770 and in design and finish could be virtually identical. High-fashion pieces by architect-designers such as Wyatt were made in Sheffield plate as well as silver. By the end of the century, the thin gauge sheet metal made in London and elsewhere, combined with the new techniques of manufacture and simple craft skills, ensured an extensive range of domestic objects from oval teapots to milk jugs, cruets, salts, sugar bowls and mustards. At the top of the London market were makers such as John Scofield and Parker & Wakelin whereas Hester Bateman and the Hennell dynasty supplied a largely middle-class clientele. The influence of the English Neo-Classical style was felt all over Europe, most obviously in Scandinavia, Russia and Portugal. Even though French style was still admired by the wealthiest foreign customers, imitations of English Adam silver were common in America, and in Italy the Valadier family created silver that shows its debt to the English interpretation of Neo-Classicism.

Swords with hilts of precious metal were worn like jewellery and reflected the owner's wealth and status: a sword was a visible indication that the wearer was a gentleman. As with other gold and silver wares, styles in swords changed and hilts were regularly melted down for their bullion value. As a result, sword-hilts of silver and especially of gold are rare before the middle of the 17th century. Hilts were usually cast from moulds and then finished by hand. Relief cast-work, piercing, chasing and engraving were the usual forms of decoration. Specialized craftsmen known as hilt-makers also supplied scabbard mounts.

By 1650 the light rapier known as a small-sword, which was worn with civilian and military dress, had become fashionable. The short sword known as a hanger or *couteau de chasse* was also fashionable in the 17th and 18th centuries. Initially used in the hunting field, these swords became widely popular, especially with naval officers. They hung vertically from the sword-belt and were very convenient when riding or travelling in coaches.

Sword-hilts of gold were worn by the very wealthy and were often presented as a reward for valour. Some of these elaborately decorated hilts are clearly the work of jewellers and gold-box makers. Firearms of fine quality were also mounted in silver and gold. Mounts usually consist of a cast butt-cap, trigger-guard and side-plate with an escutcheon in the butt for the owner's initials or arms.

Below: Gold sword-hilts were never produced in large quantities and many were melted down for their bullion value. This German small-sword dates from about 1760 and is made of three-coloured gold. It is decorated in a similar manner to contemporary gold snuff-boxes.

Opposite left: This silver-hilted English rapier dating from about 1640 is stamped with the maker's mark TH. It is rare because most silver hilts were melted down and refashioned when styles changed. As on the contemporary steel hilts it copies, the relief decoration consists of medallions and battle scenes.

Engraved designs were used by hilt-makers for very elaborate work. This design for two hilts in the advanced Rococo style of 1750 is by Jeremias Wacksmuth of Augsburg. It shows the various elements that make up a hilt: the grip, guard, pommel and scabbard-hook.

Below centre: This English hilt dating from 1676 is decorated with cast work and engraved foliage; the wooden grip is bound with silver wire. Similar hilts in brass and steel were designed for military use. The sturdy construction of this weapon suggests it was made for an officer.

Below right: Swords were sometimes mounted specially for individual customers. This English silver hanger hilt of about 1730 has been fitted with a German small-sword blade. In the late 17th and early 18th centuries exotic hardstone handles were very fashionable in England for swords and cutlery.

Right: The marking of gold and silver hilts in the 17th and 18th centuries was not properly supervised. Many hilts are unmarked or bear only a maker's mark. However on this shell-guard by the maker WB are a full set of London hallmarks and the date letter for 1676–77.

Many flintlock pistols were mounted in silver. This Irish pistol of about 1770 has a silver side-plate, trigger-guard and butt-mount. The lock is signed by the Dublin gunmaker Thomas Trulock and the silver butt-mount bears Dublin hallmarks.

REGENCY AND EMPIRE

'Foreigners from whatever part of Europe,' wrote William Rush, American Minister in London, in June 1818, 'are…struck with this profusion of solid and sumptuous plate upon English tables, as unknown in any other capital to an extent at all approaching to comparison.' Silver, either gilt or white, occupied pride of place on the tables of all who could afford it. The greatest honour the Portuguese could bestow on the Duke of Wellington, their heroic liberator, was to supply him with a monumental commemorative silver service, the Baixela da Victoria or Service of Victory (1812–16). British ambassadors, as the Crown's representatives abroad, were expected to entertain royally and were supplied with sumptuous silver services for use at state banquets and formal dinners. Those provided in 1822–3 are still in use at the Paris and Brussels embassies.

Napoleon's most sumptuous service was the Grand Vermeil, with 144 *couverts-complets* or places, which was made in 1804 by Henri Auguste. The painter Pierre-Paul Prud'hon and the architect Jacques Molinos are thought to have designed the pieces. The Grand Vermeil includes pairs of both nefs and cadenas. A nef is a ship-shaped container in which a medieval prince kept his napkin, salts and spices. Once it was placed on the royal dining table with ceremony all those present were expected to make obeisance, as though the royal person himself was at table. At the Valois court the nef was replaced by the cadenas, a locked silver casket with an attached platform, which was positioned on the king's right. He placed his cutlery and salts in the casket, and his bread and napkin on the platform. By including both nef and cadenas in the Grand Vermeil,

Napoleon consciously turned his back on the Revolution and adopted the manner of a French monarch.

Napoleon's relations revelled in their new-found royal status and ordered lavish plate to go with it. Martin-Guillaume Biennais supplied silver services to Princess Pauline Borghese (now in the Metropolitan Museum of Art, New York), and Queen Hortense of Holland. Jean-Baptiste Odiot supplied one to Jérôme Bonaparte, King of Westphalia, which is now in the Residenzmuseum, Munich. Parisian craftsmen enjoyed a reputation second to none in Europe and the Napoleonic *style empire* reigned supreme. This was largely the creation of Napoleon's two leading architects, Charles Percier and Pierre Fontaine, who published their influential designs for furniture and interiors in *Receuil de decorations interieurs* (Paris, 1802–12) and were further popularized by pattern books such as Alexandre Lefranc's *Recueil de dessins d'orfevrerie* (Paris, about 1815).

In England, men of taste like Thomas Hope, author of *Household Furniture and Interior Decoration* (London, 1807), enthusiastically adopted the new French style and the early nineteenth century was a creative period for English designers. Leading goldsmiths such as Green, Ward & Green employed the illustrator Thomas Stothard and Rundell, Bridge & Rundell employed John Flaxman as well. Charles Heathcote Tatham produced *Designs for Ornamental Plate* (London, 1806), which advocated antique ornament and 'massiveness', as opposed to the 'light and insignificant' designs associated with Robert Adam. In spite of continual war from 1803 until 1815, Britain prospered:

REGENCY FETE or John Bull in the Conservatory.

The Prince Regent's appetite for extravagant silvergilt dinner plate provoked this 1811 cartoon.

Tatham could assure the aspiring 'young Chaser' that in this 'rich, liberal and enlightened country', hard work and perseverance brought ample reward.

A silver service consisted of a great many entrée and dessert plates and corresponding sets of flatware. For example, amongst the entrée plate in the Duke of Wellington's ambassadorial service issued by the Jewel House in August 1814 were four tureens, four candelabra, 12 dozen table plates and a large centre ornament. His dessert plate of gilt included a dozen fruit dishes, two dozen matching plates and six dozen knives, forks and spoons. The dessert was regarded as the most important part of the dinner – hence the widespread use of silvergilt plate which was more costly and a greater compliment to the user.

From about 1800 heavier and more expensive items

of silver were included in the service, the largest and longest of which was the plateau. Originally a support for a centrepiece, it was highly suitable as an elongated ornament for the long table, which by then dominated the dining room. The glow of the silver and candles was enhanced by a mirror plate that formed the base. Examples of such pieces include the Gothic Alnwick plateau, designed by the Duchess of Northumberland and executed by Edward Thomason, and the Earl of Belmore's plateau with three tripod dessert stands to a design of Thomas Hope and executed by Paul Storr (1810, Al-Tajir Collection). Perhaps the grandest plateau of this period in any European collection is that in the Baixela da Victoria (see above), the masterpiece of Portugal's leading painter Domingos Antonio de Sequeira. He is known to have sought out the latest

English patterns, including Tatham's design for a plateau presented to Lord Nelson to commemorate the battle of the Nile, although he ended up borrowing a number of French motifs, such as Charles Percier's griffin candelabra.

Amongst the most lavish English plateaux were those supplied by Rundell, Bridge & Rundell to the Prince Regent. They included one with six reliefs depicting the arts and the sciences that cost £1,681; another large and superb one with the arms and trophies of Edward the Black Prince cost £693 for supplementary ornaments (in the form of helmets, flags, cross bows and other devices) alone. The Prince Regent ordered eight large ice pails modelled on the Warwick Vase at the hefty sum of £2,895 and a 'richly chased Sideboard dish...with the Devises of the Feast of the Gods, from a design of Michael Angelo'. In addition to the Black Prince plateau, the royal goldsmiths Rundell, Bridge & Rundell supplied him with a 'curious chased Silver Tankard, with chased Figure of Henry the Eighth'. The Prince Regent was not alone in his antiquarian interest. William Beckford's sideboard furniture at Fonthill in Wiltshire was 'revived Renaissance' and he ordered a set of 'Jacobethan' revival sconces from William Burwash in 1818. His love of sixteenth-century strapwork and moresque was quite out of step with Tathamesque 'massiveness'.

An expensive service ordered from the Jewel House was that for Sir Charles Stewart, when he left for the Berlin embassy in 1813. The white silver cost £3,241 and the silvergilt £666. It is modest, however, when compared with the large service of silver loaned and shipped to the Prince Regent of Portugal in Brazil in 1815. This consignment included candlesticks, plateaux, epergnes, bread baskets and ice pails, as well as tea services complete with urns, kettles, sugar basins and cream ewers.

Elaborate etiquette accompanied the use of these grand services, although after about 1810 the elegant *service à la française* was gradually replaced by what was considered to be the more practical *service à la russe*. In *service à la française* all dishes were laid symmetrically on the table for diners to help themselves, and each couvert consisted of a large plate in the centre, with dishes at the side and triangular ones in the corners of the table. The fact that the Baixela da Victoria originally contained some 24 triangular dishes indicates that Sequeira was still thinking in terms of *service à la française*. This custom prevailed as late as 1826 in grand circles in England. According to Prince Puckler-Muskau, 'everyman helps himself from the dish already in front of him and offers it to his neighbour. If he wants something extra, he must either ask across the table for it or send a servant in search of it.' He found this a tiresome custom, but added, 'those who have been abroad have adopted the more convenient German practise of having dishes handed round by the servants.'

The new European practice of servants passing along the table and serving from different dishes from a sideboard had long been the Russian custom. Martha Wilmot who visited Russia between 1803 and 1808 disliked such arrangements: 'many a bad dinner have I made from the mere fatigue of [there] being fifty or sixty different Dishes by servant who come one after the other and flourish ready carv'd fish, flesh, fowl, vegetables, fruits, soups of fish.' Nevertheless, the practice prevailed, with the result that most of the plate was gradually banished from the table to the sideboard, leaving the table centre free of plateaux, vases of flowers and candelabra.

Above: The spout in the form of a panther and the moon-shaped tap complete the Classical vocabulary of this coffee vase.
Opposite: Nymphs dancing around a candelabrum; part of the Duke of Wellington's centrepiece, Lisbon, 1815.

The silver holdings of most public institutions are made up of objects assembled from many sources at different times. Generally speaking, it is rare for collections to remain intact although there are notable exceptions, such as the 16th-century collections of the Wittelsbach family held in the Residenzmuseum in Munich and the famous Grünes Gewölbe (Green Vaults) in Dresden, home to the collections of the Electors of Saxony.

Silver has always been at risk of being melted down when money was short, or requisitioned by a needy ruler, and equally likely to be remade as fashions change. Wars and religious upheavals have also had a great impact: the Thirty Years War, the French Revolution and the Napoleonic Wars were all responsible for the loss or dispersal of large amounts of silver. The Reformation and the liturgical revivals in its wake triggered a demand for replacement church plate. From the early 18th century connoisseurship was a powerful stimulus to the market as antiquarian collectors such as William Beckford and Horace Walpole became interested in old plate.

Below: This group of objects from William Beckford's famous collection at Fonthill in Wiltshire includes a medieval enamel reliquary casket from the Treasury of the Abbey of St Denis in Paris, described by John Evelyn in 1643 as 'one of the richest in Plate, Jewels, Shrines, Reliques etc in Europ'. In common with many other ecclesiastical collections in France, it was stripped during the Revolution.

Economic realities for such institutions as guilds and colleges brought silver on to the market in the 19th century. The Nuremberg goldsmiths' guild, for example, sold its silver in 1868, ostensibly for the benefit of 'widows and orphans', but probably to balance its books.

The objects here illustrate some of the ways that silver has arrived on the market or found its way through different collections into the Victoria and Albert Museum.

The significance of this English political cartoon of 1805, 'The Plumb Pudding in Danger', lies in the illustration of the disruptive effect of the Napoleonic Wars. The predatory activities of William Pitt and Napoleon had social and artistic as well as political repercussions, which resulted in the loss and dispersal of silver. France and Italy were particularly badly affected.

Below: The splendid gilt ewer and basin are unmarked but were probably made in Paris about 1580. Described as 'Cellini silver', they were acquired by George, third Earl Cowper on his Grand Tour in Florence about 1765. Like the famous Lomellini ewer and basin (see 'Mannerism'), they illustrate the antiquarian interest and taste for spectacular Mannerist silver of a section of the English aristocracy.

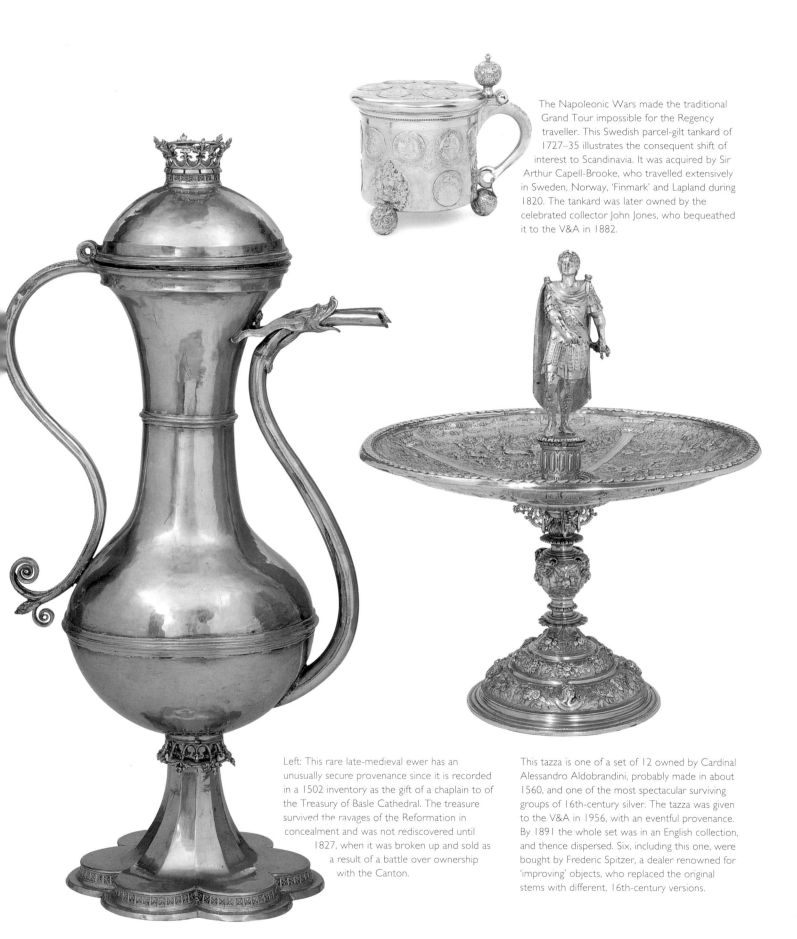

The Napoleonic Wars made the traditional Grand Tour impossible for the Regency traveller. This Swedish parcel-gilt tankard of 1727–35 illustrates the consequent shift of interest to Scandinavia. It was acquired by Sir Arthur Capell-Brooke, who travelled extensively in Sweden, Norway, 'Finmark' and Lapland during 1820. The tankard was later owned by the celebrated collector John Jones, who bequeathed it to the V&A in 1882.

Left: This rare late-medieval ewer has an unusually secure provenance since it is recorded in a 1502 inventory as the gift of a chaplain to of the Treasury of Basle Cathedral. The treasure survived the ravages of the Reformation in concealment and was not rediscovered until 1827, when it was broken up and sold as a result of a battle over ownership with the Canton.

This tazza is one of a set of 12 owned by Cardinal Alessandro Aldobrandini, probably made in about 1560, and one of the most spectacular surviving groups of 16th-century silver. The tazza was given to the V&A in 1956, with an eventful provenance. By 1891 the whole set was in an English collection, and thence dispersed. Six, including this one, were bought by Frederic Spitzer, a dealer renowned for 'improving' objects, who replaced the original stems with different, 16th-century versions.

ECLECTICISM

Eclecticism was not a new phenomenon. The Italian Renaissance had rediscovered Classicism, the Rococo drew on grotesques and the late eighteenth and early nineteenth centuries saw Gothic, Greek, Roman and Egyptian revivals. But it was in the four decades after 1820 that eclecticism was most enthusiastically embraced, combining absolute zeal for diverse historic, naturalistic and exotic styles with an energetic and creative approach. The variety of interpretations ranged from the strictly archaeological plate of A.W.N. Pugin to the romanticized and imaginative designs of William Burges. The systematic comparative study of design, as in Owen Jones's *Grammar of Ornament* (1856), and the attempts to codify design theory by Henry Cole and others (see 'Design Reform in England') helped to fuel the consumers' awareness of stylistic diversity. The commercial silver trade was able and eager to supply the increasing demand for affordable silver in any historic style the customer wished.

Fascination with the past sprang from many roots. Nationalism, which arose in Spain, the Netherlands, in Belgium after 1831 and the German states after the Napoleonic era was partly responsible. The energy of architects, poets, artists and novelists such as Sir Walter Scott fostered an atmosphere in which several historic styles could flourish concurrently. The linked appetites of antiquaries and connoisseur–collectors also played a role. A privately negotiated dispersal of old English royal silver in 1808, much of it late Stuart buffet plate and sconces, provided furnishing silver for the houses of the Earl of Lonsdale, the Duke of Buccleuch and the Brownlow family at Belton House in Lincolnshire. As collections of historic silver came on to the market,

notably those of the Duke of Norfolk (1816), the Duke of York (1827) and the Duke of Chandos and Buckingham (1848), more examples of past styles were offered. In the absence of museums, salerooms were one of the few places where historic applied art objects could be seen.

The most prestigious and influential silversmiths of early nineteenth-century England were the royal goldsmiths Rundell, Bridge & Rundell. In 1803 they had executed a royal commission to supply matching pieces to a marine service in the Rococo style by Nicholas Sprimont. A decade later they supplied sideboard dishes chased in the seventeenth-century floral taste for the royal dukes and in the mid-1820s they produced presentation cups in a romanticized medieval manner. Through their aristocratic clients, they had direct access to old plate and their lead in the reintroduction and reinterpretation of historic style was often decisive. Their ability to market costly and sophisticated plate in a number of styles was unmatched by their competitors and their showrooms educated potential purchasers as well as other retailers. The quality of their designers, who included the artist and sculptor John Flaxman, as well as the proficiency and skill of the workshops run by Paul Storr and Benjamin Smith, ensured that Rundell's maintained pre-eminence in the trade for over 20 years. The cost of maintaining a large design studio was not possible for every manufacturer, particularly those serving the wider market.

The Rococo, which was at first the advanced taste of a small élite, including Rundell's greatest patron, the Prince Regent (later George IV), became the most persistent and long-lived of the revived styles. In a more

Tureen combining Gothic and Classical elements, designed by Karl Friedrich Schinkel,
1842–47 and made by Hossauer, Berlin.

ornate, bulbous and heavily sinuous form than the original version of the 1740s and '50s, it attracted a great deal of unfavourable criticism. By the 1830s the French were dismayed by the appearance of what they termed the 'English style', an uneasy mix of Renaissance and Rococo, in the work of their goldsmiths. The Rococo revival was also attacked by a select committee appointed by Parliament in 1835 to enquire into and improve the current state of design. Manufacturers and artists joined with government officials to condemn its repetitious and unoriginal nature, and yet the industry in Birmingham and Sheffield continued to produce wares in the style that as Louis-Quatorze or Louis-Quinze remained the most frequent choice of an aspiring middle class throughout the nineteenth century.

Rundell's were not alone in designing and selling plate in historic styles. Lambert & Rawlings and Kensington Lewis were two retailers who sold interesting romanticized plate in old styles as well as genuinely old or improved pieces to which chasing had been added. Books of designs, such as *Knight's Vases and Ornaments* (1833), were intended to assist manufacturers' choice of ornament and form. In France, manufacturers like Charles Wagner experimented with past techniques. He has been credited with reviving niello decoration in Europe and with encouraging the reintroduction in France of enamelling and the use of jewels to add colour and richness to silver. The Marrel brothers, accomplished silversmiths in this type of work, produced a covered cup in 1839 that was shown at the Great Exhibition of 1851. It was judged to be of sufficient quality to be purchased for the fledgling Victoria and Albert Museum as an example worthy of emulation. In England, such decorative techniques were confined almost exclusively to the proponents of the Medieval movement.

One of the earliest examples of the revived interest in a medieval style was the National Cup designed by Flaxman in 1819 and made by Rundell's for George IV in 1824–25. A.W.N. Pugin, whose career began with designing for Rundell's in a similarly romantic Gothic taste, was to become the sternest critic of this kind of stylistic inaccuracy. That the Gothic style became the main focus for innovation was due almost entirely to Pugin. He studied the ecclesiastical plate of fourteenth- and fifteenth-century Europe and went into partnership with the Birmingham manufacturer John Hardman junior in 1838 to produce furnishings, largely for the church. Pugin's Medieval Court at the Great Exhibition won a Council Medal for the range and quality of Hardman's metalwork, a tribute to an enterprise that pragmatically mixed new industrial techniques such as electrogilding with the more traditional craft-based skills of raising and chasing. By 1862, when the fashion for the Gothic was at its height, even teapots and toast racks were decorated with trefoils and foliated arches. The Gothic continued to inspire designers such as William Burges (1827–81) whose designs owed more to an antiquarian interest in the medieval period than a commitment to authenticity.

Although the collector William Beckford had ordered plate in the revived Renaissance style as early as 1816, it did not become popular in England until it was supported by Prince Albert and promoted by Henry Cole and others through the Schools of Design. This was not true of France, where admiration for the Renaissance ensured that the style had remained part of designers' and manufacturers' repertoire. Examples from the work of the best exponents such as F.J. Rudolphi and F.D. Froment-Meurice were bought by the Schools of Design and for the Victoria and Albert Museum's early collections. Very few English designers, apart from Alfred Stevens, successfully mastered the use of Renaissance ornament. Many firms relied upon foreign and largely French artists. Antoine Vechte, a chaser of great renown, worked from 1849 to 1862 for Hunt & Roskell, one of the foremost silversmithing firms of the mid-nineteenth century, and produced a series of virtuoso pieces. G.R. Elkington employed several French designers, including Vechte's former pupil Leonard Morel-Ladeuil (1820–88), and their work dominated the firm's stands at international exhibitions between 1862 and 1873.

The Neo-Classical style never really went out of fashion although it was briefly eclipsed in the 1830s and '40s by the Rococo revival. In Germany the archi-

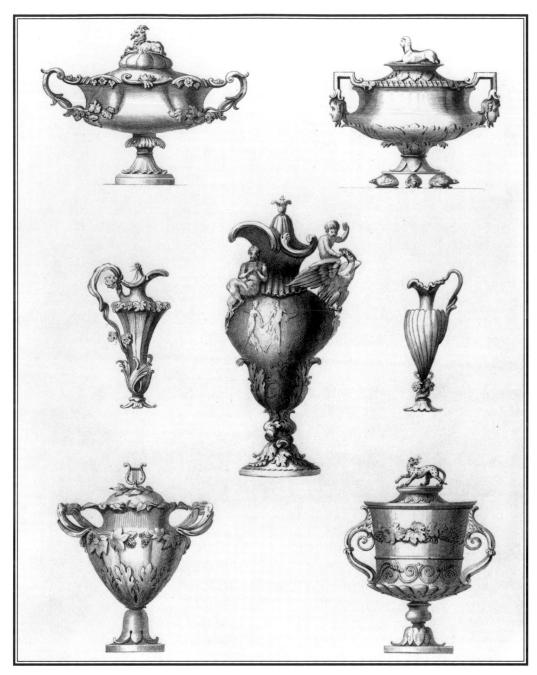

A page from *Knight's Vases and Ornaments* (1833), published to provide models for silversmiths.

tect Karl Friedrich Schinkel, who thought that Classicism and the Gothic could be complementary, did not hesitate to marry teutonic knights with Classical forms and motifs. The Rococo revival, with its playful use of natural forms, increased the enthusiasm for employing nature as a decorative device on art objects. Designers such as Flaxman and Thomas Stothard looked to nature for inspiration. It was not long before the addition of decorative foliage or flowers had enveloped the whole structure of the object. At its best naturalism could be strikingly original, but as it evolved in English silver it soon came to mean drowning form and function in decorative excess. Although the 1835 committee had approved of naturalism and Henry Cole had recommended it as a good stylistic model, by 1851 and the Great Exhibition criticism was mounting. Naturalism was vilified in France as another example of an unwelcome English influence. In the principles of design theory set out by Henry Cole and his teachers at the art schools, the importance of appropriate ornament, subservient to an object's function, was emphasized.

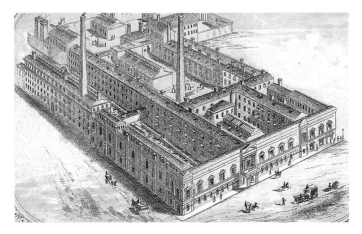

There are from time to time novelties introduced into manufactures so startling that it is difficult at first to regard them in the sober light of industrial processes; since they seem to belong rather to the marvellous than to the real. Who would have thought, for instance, of a silver vase or candelabrum, or any other article of table-plate, being made through the agency of electricity?

THE PENNY MAGAZINE, OCTOBER 1844

To the Victorians it seemed almost magical that silver could be made through the action of electricity. The principal techniques developed were electroplating, where silver could be deposited on to a base metal by the action of an electric current; electrotyping, which used a similar means to form the whole object; and electrogilding, which replaced the more hazardous mercury gilding.

The successful development of these processes and the marketing of electroplate as a cheaper substitute for silver must be credited to George Richard Elkington (1800–65) and his cousin and partner Henry Elkington (about 1810–52). The

commercial use of earlier experiments with electrometallurgy began with the patent taken out by the Elkingtons in 1840. The cousins were not inventors as such but innovators who, by applying the processes to an industry, revolutionized the silver and plating trades all over the world. Licences to make the new products were sold widely in England and abroad to firms such as Christofle & Co. in Paris. Within ten years the market for Sheffield plate was collapsing and electroplate, which was prominently displayed on the Elkington stand at the 1851 Great Exhibition, had won respectability and acceptance, even in high society and the art world.

By the 1860s Elkington's was the largest firm in the English trade and their factory in Birmingham (above left) employed about 1,000 workers. The site was the main focus of the electroplating activities, which included the ornamental and artistic work. The factory's improved plating dynamo (above right) could deposit 50 ounces of silver an hour. It is shown serving the vats into which objects for plating were suspended. The oval stamp (below left) was applied from 1853 to electrotypes officially approved by the Science and Art Department.

To retain their prestige in the commercial world, Elkington's continued to make large and elaborate exhibition pieces of fine-quality silver. The cost of producing them was recouped by the sale of electrotype copies.

The bulk of Elkington's business was supplying the market for small domestic items in silver or electroplate in a range of styles from Egyptian to Neo-Classical. This page from one of the factory pattern books shows the diversity of salt cellars available to retailers.

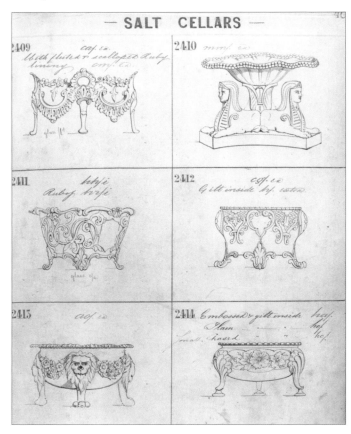

The large electrotypes of lions were replicated from original silver models in the Castle of Rosenborg in Denmark. They were made as part of a programme led by the South Kensington Museum to create copies of historic silver objects. There was high demand for these electrotypes as examples of good design from museums all over the world. Much of the work was done by Elkington's.

The card case in electroplated nickel silver, which has been partly gilded, was designed for Elkington's by George Stanton. Made in 1852, it was shown at several international exhibitions as an example of good modern design in the Renaissance style.

Left: Pugin's Medieval Court at the Great Exhibition, 1851.

Below: As part of his campaign for good design, Henry Cole began a business in 1847 under the pseudonym of Felix Summerly. He aimed to bring together established artists and adventurous manufacturers to produce 'pretty objects of everyday use'. The products had limited financial success but acted as a focus for design reform.

'Silver-work has sunk to a mere trade, and art is rigidly excluded from its arrangements.' A.W.N. Pugin expressed a widely shared concern with the low standard of English silver design in the 1830s and '40s. Unlike other European countries, England had no tradition of state involvement with the promotion of design and artisans had little or no formal training. Anxiety about competition with France led Parliament in 1835 to appoint two select committees to suggest improvements. These recommended that schools of design and a museum of approved design be opened to educate artisans, manufacturers and consumers. Equally significant was the creation of the Patent Design Registry in 1842 for the protection of designs against piracy.

Henry Cole (1808–82), an energetic civil servant, arranged exhibitions of art manufactures at the Society of Arts under the patronage of its president, Prince Albert. These culminated in the Great Exhibition of 1851 which was intended 'to extend the Influence of Science and Art upon Productive Industry'. Large English silversmiths such as Barnard's and Elkington's led the world in technical innovation and manufacturing skill, and had extensive export business, but seemed unable to reconcile the benefits of mechanization with traditional hand skills and inventive design. In 1851 critics compared British plate unfavourably with German and French products. At the International Exhibition of 1862 it was conceded that England had achieved some success but the difficulty of generating, producing and marketing good design could not easily be resolved. The silver trade became polarized between traditionally made objects, especially testimonials by firms such as Hancock's (founded 1849), and everyday silver and electroplate from Sheffield and Birmingham. Few designers from the official Schools of Design were able to realize the potential of machine production. Christopher Dresser (1834–1904), a product of the Kensington School of Design (now the Royal College of Art), was an honourable and influential exception.

The international exhibitions encouraged virtuoso displays of design and craftsmanship which added to the prestige of the manufacturers. Many English firms turned to foreign designers. Leonard Morel-Ladeuil, the French artist and chaser of the Milton Shield, was one of the most skilful chasers of the period.

The European appetite for presentation silver stimulated weighty and elaborate pieces. From the 1860s these became more stylized, overladen and ungainly in design. The Sir Moses Montefiore Testimonial (1842) with its well-modelled figures and balanced design represents the best of the presentation class.

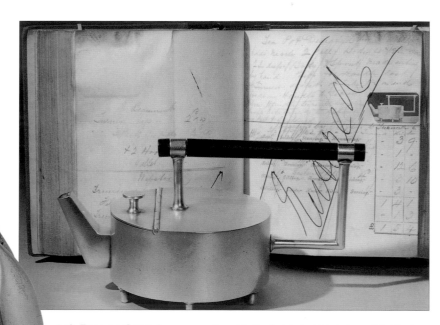

Left: This large Gothic flagon was made for the Great Exhibition by C.T. & G. Fox. Although it had no practical purpose, it was bought for the founding collection of the V&A in 1852, at a cost of £128 8s., as an example of good design and craftsmanship.

Arguably the first industrial designer, Christopher Dresser demonstrated a rare ability to exploit new technology in the manufacture of silver and electroplate. His successful designs for Hukin & Heath, based on the Victorian interest in geometric and oriental forms, were simple and functional. This prototype teapot was, however, too costly to be manufactured.

THE DILEMMA OF THE 1890s: OLD OR NEW?

The appeal of silver was already faltering in the late nineteenth century, due to competition from cheaper alternatives, and the market for it was dividing. Those who liked old silver could find it: 'we rummage Lambert's or Carrington's for real old Georgian silver punch bowls to use as centrepieces' (1891). Admirers of the self-consciously handmade could patronize Essex House, C.R. Ashbee's London premises, or go to the retailers Connell's or Liberty's for modern artistic silver-ware that was produced by machine but with a handmade look. The traditional demand continued for plate chests, flatware or wedding presents and what Anthony Trollope called 'an elaborate coffee-pot, which in spite of its inutility and ugliness' was valued for its donor's sake, but, judging from the advertisements of retailers such as Savory & Son of Cornhill, or the Goldsmiths' and Silversmiths' Alliance, these goods had little vitality or originality of design. A feeble Queen Anne style, called 'colonial revival' in North America, suited contemporary Georgian interior decoration. For those patrons excited by the Aesthetic movement, there was also the love affair with Japanese forms and motifs that flourished from the 1870s to 1900.

Silver was for the English a costly pleasure. All the raw material had to be imported (or recycled), there was duty of 1s. 6d an ounce until 1890 and an excellent alternative in electroplate. The difference in price was considerable. When Ashbee started offering plated versions of his Guild of Handicraft designs, the muffin dish cost only £2 or £3 whereas a silver version cost five times as much.

After the rigidities of design reform and the tyranny of the South Kensington system in the mid-nineteenth century, there was a refreshing new emphasis on craft skill and tradition at the colleges in the 1890s. Crafts were seen as worthwhile and uplifting and open to amateurs as well as professionals. An alternative was sought to the traditional trade apprenticeship and C.R. Ashbee prided himself on not employing silversmiths from the trade, 'such experience was...regarded rather as a detriment'. This dilemma, the seesaw between design and craft in silver has characterized the past 100 years. But it is in effect an artificial dilemma, since potential purchasers probably appreciate both approaches. Handwork found an extreme expression and marketing device in the Martelé silver of the Gorham Company, heavy handworked pieces each raised from a single sheet.

Although it is fashionable to dismiss late nineteenth-century silver, there was a lively inventiveness in smaller wares such as dressing table sets, smoking para-phernalia or christening sets. Ireland and Scandinavia were both struggling for a sense of national identity reflected in silver. Shamrocks had cropped up on seven-teenth-century Irish chalices and were incorporated into the chasing of Dublin-made baskets by Robert Calderwood in the middle of the eighteenth century. But a richer and more comprehensive vocabulary of interlace, stylized animal forms and inset stones charac-terizes Irish silver after the 1850s. In Oslo the dragon style flourished a little later and included traditional enamelwork, as well as themes from Nordic myths.

The English, French and German trades were inevitably driven by the economics of large-scale production. There were 160 factories in Germany in 1900 but 'few...were willing to risk overly complicated

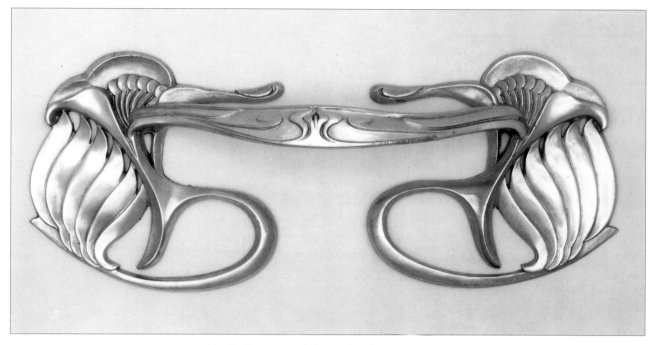

Handle from a set of electroplate furniture mounts.

artistic experiments with such a commercially sensitive material.' Both public and craftsmen liked long-established, reassuring shapes carrying the weight of tradition. Technical investment in new moulds and patterns was costly and had to be reclaimed over a reasonably long period of production. All these factors worked together to hold back new designs. Between 1870 and 1900 manufacturers imitated Japanese mixed metal effects and exploited Japanese artefacts such as the bamboo fans taken as models for teatrays by Elkington's (1879, Patent Design registered 1880). Aldwinkle & Slater's three bears for condiments were well-made, heavy and usable and had a market appeal because of their small size and relatively low cost in duty. Art nouveau influenced English manufacturers such as Huttons of Sheffield and the vitality of whiplash motifs appealed to sophisticated purchasers, despite criticism of the 1900 Paris exhibition by English reviewers.

In flatware, too, the manufacturers could offer an astonishing variety of more or less elaborate dies. A pattern book of the old London spoon-makers, Chawners, assembled about 1875, includes more than

47 variant for handmade flatware: Elizabethan, New Gothic, Rossetti, Dolphin, Cambridge, Paxton, Plantagenet.... From the 1840s the Sheffield industry was predominant, producing machine-made flatware to a price. Even these were undercut by electroplate. In 1847 a set of Elkington's tableforks cost £2 4s. whereas 12 silver forks would be £15 or more.

The most striking change in the English pattern of ownership of silver was at the top of society. Between the 1870s and the First World War a quiet revolution had taken place. The gradual disappearance of the landed classes destroyed a way of life of which silver had always been a symbol. The sale of silver had always been a convenient means of raising capital, for example when executors had to clear debts. Large display plate, such as the cistern and fountain sold by Lord Romney in 1704 or the Lamerie cooler, made for the fourth Earl of Scarsdale and sold on his death to the Tsarina Anna, was bought by fellow aristocrats and circulated within a long-established pattern. In addition to inherited or second-hand English silver, the Duke of Buccleuch, the Duke of Devonshire, the Duke of Sussex or the Duke of Hamilton had amassed magnificent collections of old Continental silver in the first half of the nineteenth century. But the economic squeeze of the 1880s and later, which forced works of art out on to the market, coincided with the new transatlantic phenomenon of the industrialist–collector. Family possessions were seen as investments rather than heirlooms.

The modern international art market, now so familiar, is barely a century old. When the Elizabethan mounted porcelain (now in the Metropolitan Museum of Art) was sold from Burghley House in 1888, J.P. Morgan was already in the market and Duveen bought silver at the Anson sale in 1893. The Irish aristocracy was hit particularly hard. By the 1920s there were virtually no large Irish estates left and their works of art, including silver, were scattered. The Kildare toilet service, bought in 1926 for the Wernher Collection, has at last returned to Ireland (Ulster Museum, Belfast).

Unease about this new American market, or threat as it was seen, prompted the creation of the National Art Collections Fund in 1903. A parallel unease was growing about sales of historic plate by churches. Secular silver of the late sixteenth and seventeenth centuries, particularly flagons, rosewater basins and cups, given over the years to beautify worship, were being replaced from the 1830s by new Gothic plate, regarded as more fitting. Antique dealers competed for these old church pieces, since there was very little other domestic plate available to satisfy collectors. After a proposed sale to an American collector led to a passionate public

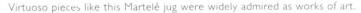

Virtuoso pieces like this Martelé jug were widely admired as works of art.

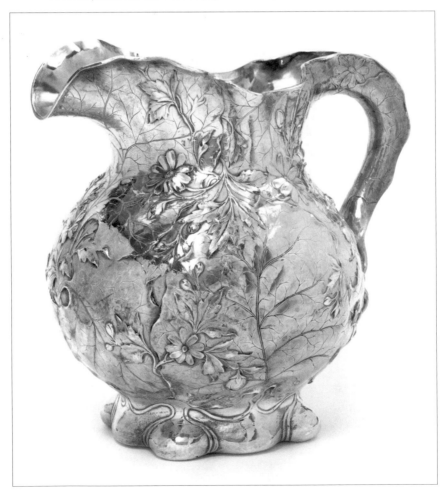

Late 19th-century flatware in the popular Japanese style made by selected American manufacturers.

campaign articulated in the letter pages of *The Times*, the Victoria and Albert Museum set up the first Church Plate Loan Gallery in 1914. The object that had triggered the outcry, the medieval Studley Bowl, had been given to that Yorkshire church only a generation before. Church sales of plate were virtually unregulated: the plate manufacturer and dealer George Lambert had accumulated in the course of trade so large a group of Elizabethan communion cups that he was able to present 12 to the Goldsmiths' Company.

Fakes inevitably flourished alongside the new enthusiasm for old silver. Old objects were improved by adding chasing or marks and new pieces were marked to deceive. Even contemporary historicist plate could later acquire misleading old marks, as happened with the firm of Bossard in Lucerne.

Left: Silversmiths specializing in small inexpensive novelties such as nutmeg graters, boxes and propelling pencils were often referred to as 'toymakers', not because the objects were for children but because of their size. Henry Manton made among other things such refined toilet accessories as ear scoops, illustrated in the bottom right of this trade card.

Right: The German firm WMF, founded in 1853 with a workshop of 16, expanded by 1914 to a veritable taskforce of 6,000 exporting fashionable art-nouveau electroplated and silver tableware world-wide. The demand from the English market was so great that in 1908 Wurttemberg House, a large showroom on the edge of Holborn Viaduct, employed 30 people.

On 13 February 1511 a masque was held at Westminster Palace for which the court goldsmith Robert Amadas supplied gold novelties in the form of hearts and initials (259 H's, 218 K's). They were sewn on to Henry VIII's costume to be 'given by the King to lords and ladies off his jacket' as frivolous keepsakes. One rare survivor, perhaps given on a similar occasion and by family tradition a gift from Henry VIII to Anne Boleyn, is on display at the V&A. It is a small gold whistle beautifully engraved with flowers and, in true Swiss army style, contains miniature folding cosmetic tools. Specialist 'smallworkers' or 'toymen' had their own marks and trade outlets. The taste for small novelties in precious metal continues to the present.

Novel forms sprang from new materials. The introduction of meerschaum, a soft opaque mineral that is easily worked, to England in the 18th century led to a fashion for highly and often amusingly carved meerschaum pipes. Hyam Hyams used the popularity

of this novelty to advertise the goods that he had recently bought from the Duke of Sussex's sale in 1843: 'Massive gold-mounted Meerschaum Pipe, constantly used by his late Royal highness' (*Illustrated London News*).

Even in the 19th and early 20th centuries when Sheffield plate and electroplate dominated the mass market, novelties were still made in precious metals, mostly silver, because their small size and largely mechanized manufacture kept prices low. Silversmiths in

Birmingham and Sheffield cornered the market producing quirky pieces based on animals, flowers and amusing larger-than-life characters such as Punch.

These women worked for J.W. Evans of Birmingham, founded in 1880, which supplied unfinished silver and plated tableware to large retailers such as Mappin & Webb and Walker & Hall. Like many suppliers their work was anonymous until, to celebrate their centenary, the present director John Evans registered a mark at the Birmingham Assay Office in 1980. The firm still supplies major retailing outlets.

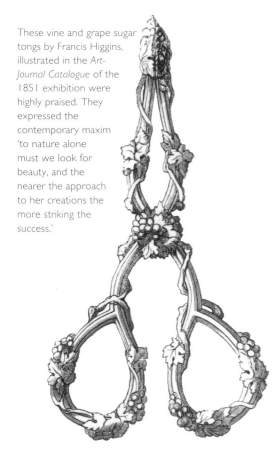

These vine and grape sugar tongs by Francis Higgins, illustrated in the *Art-Journal Catalogue* of the 1851 exhibition were highly praised. They expressed the contemporary maxim 'to nature alone must we look for beauty, and the nearer the approach to her creations the more striking the success.'

Pocket knives, étuis, boot hooks, tobacco tampers and boxes for pills and stamps were typical of the smallwork on Henry Manton's trade card. Such goods were made by specialists, often outworkers.

This decorative inkstand with tree trunk taperstick and containers for ink, sand and wafers disguised as fruits exemplifies the twin Victorian obsessions with naturalism and historicism. The design was copied from a mid-18th century Dutch object.

Even the naturalistic 'branch' supports of this Arts and Crafts fancy by Benson & Webb (London, 1890) are silver. A less grand brass and copper version of the gypsy kettle and stand could be purchased in 1902 for 26s. 6d from the Army and Navy Store.

The elements of Modernism first emerged in the silver designed by C.R. Ashbee, the pre-eminent Arts and Crafts designer of silver and jewellery, and produced by his Guild of Handicraft at the turn of the century. Modernism had its ideological basis in functionalism, expressed through an abstract purity which, at its most extreme, eliminated entirely all extraneous ornament. The restrained austerity and formal elegance of Ashbee's designs had considerable influence abroad, most notably on Josef Hoffmann and his work for the Wiener Werkstätte. The 1925 Exposition des Arts Décoratifs et Industriels in Paris demonstrated conclusively that progressive, modernistic silver design came from the heart of Europe and most notably from France. Silversmiths such as Jean Puiforçat and Jean Tétard displayed work with a strong geometric character in which superfluous ornamentation had been pared away in the pursuit of a predominantly functional form. The only real concession to ornament was the incorporation of costly materials such as rare woods, ivory, hardstones and crystal. Several individual jewellers, among them Jean Després and Gérard Sandoz, and the jewellery houses of Cartier, Van Cleef & Arpels, for example, were inspired to produce silver in the new style. Sandoz produced a limited number of distinctive objects with details of lizard skin and ivory. British silversmiths began to be receptive to these influences in the 1930s. On the whole, they exercised more restraint than their continental colleagues although some of the most innovative, such as H.G. Murphy, were their equal.

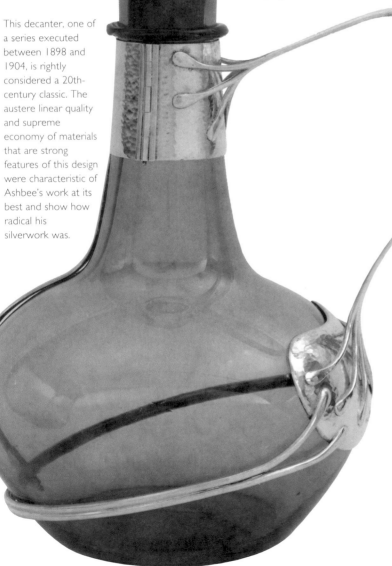

This decanter, one of a series executed between 1898 and 1904, is rightly considered a 20th-century classic. The austere linear quality and supreme economy of materials that are strong features of this design were characteristic of Ashbee's work at its best and show how radical his silverwork was.

Gleadowe (1888–1944), art master at Winchester College and Slade Professor at Oxford, was one of the ablest designers to work with silversmiths in the 1930s. His earlier work, such as on the Sea Beaker illustrated here, was marked by detailed pictorial engraving and later, particularly when he and Murphy collaborated, by plainer services with fluting and curved outlines.

Jean Puiforçat (1897–1945), the son of a goldsmith, was largely self-taught as a designer although he did study sculpture under Louis Lejeune. An independent goldsmith after 1922, he became famous for his geometric style which he always claimed had its basis in mathematics. He was prominently displayed and much admired at the Paris exhibitions of 1925 and 1937.

Above: This tea service was developed by H.G. Murphy as a prototype for industrial manufacture. Handwork was reduced to the minimum: the bodies are made up of die-stamped halves joined by a simple fold-over seam; the lids detach to eliminate the need for hinges. Although the service won a prize at the Milan Exhibition of 1933 and was exhibited at the V&A in 1934, no manufacturer was willing to put it into production.

Below: Harold Stabler (1872–1945), a founder member of the Design and Industries Association (DIA), was one of the most important British silversmiths of the inter-war years. He was one of the close advisers to Frank Pick, the Chief Executive of the London Passenger Transport Board and a fellow member of the DIA. In the late 1930s the inventors of stainless steel, Firth Vickers, commissioned Stabler to develop a series of prototypes in the new material but no British manufacturer was interested in producing them. They were subsequently made in Scandinavia.

THE IMPACT OF MODERNISM

★JULY 4TH. TO 16TH.

THE HALL-MARK OF THE WORSHIPFUL COMPANY OF GOLDSMITHS

EXHIBITION OF MODERN SILVERWORK GOLDSMITHS' HALL FOSTER LANE E.C.2 OPEN 10 A.M.TILL 7·30.P.M. ADMISSION FREE

Exhibitions arranged by the Goldsmiths' Company have been one of the most successful means of promoting new work and ideas.

The work of Charles Robert Ashbee (1863–1942) and his Guild of Handicraft had a dramatic and immediate influence on the design and development of European and American twentieth-century metalwork design. Ashbee, who trained as an architect, was strongly attracted to the ideals of William Morris (1834–1906). They were both committed to the goals of the Arts and Crafts movement which sought to revive the role of the individual artist/craftsman. The Guild of Handicraft, prompted by the example of William Morris and the influential writings of the critic John Ruskin, was established by Ashbee in 1888 as a nineteenth-century concept of a medieval craft workshop. Early work by the Guild was comparatively crude and amateurish, but Ashbee and his colleagues learnt quickly through a programme of self-education that was wholly devised by Ashbee. Interestingly, this drew heavily on the opportunities to study and handle objects offered by the South Kensington Museum (now the Victoria and Albert Museum). Ashbee was not averse to drawing on historical precedent, but the style of silverwork and jewellery that the Guild produced at the turn of the century was both innovative and original, relying on a simple and austere use of form and colour. Soft curves,

a deliberately dull finish to the metal and the discreet use of semi-precious stones and monochrome enamel perfectly exploited the limitations both of Ashbee's craftsmen and the material. The result was a series of objects exhibiting a subtle modernity which radically redefined the aesthetic and tradition of working in precious metals.

Although the Arts and Crafts Society and Ashbee in particular enjoyed considerable prestige abroad, the Guild was short-lived. When Ashbee found that others were adopting his ideas and exploiting them commercially, he was forced to close the Guild. Younger men such as Henry Wilson, Alexander Fisher and Arthur Gaskin were beginning to produce work that was richer, more self-assured and stylish than the austere simplicity of the Guild of Handicraft. Insofar as this was the work of small individual craft workshops, Ashbee could only approve; but he was irritated by the major retailer Liberty initiating its Cymric silver range in 1899, which was produced on a semi-industrial basis by Hasler's of Birmingham. The Cymric style was a rich blend of Arts and Crafts mannerisms and continental art nouveau. Early designs in particular were largely supplied by Archibald Knox and owed a considerable debt to Ashbee and his Guild of Handicraft.

Dell, along with Moholy-Nagy, was in charge of the Bauhaus metal workshops during their most productive period.

At the turn of the century the British were in the forefront of the European avant-garde, but it was not a position that they were to retain. Even at the height of its authority in the mid-1890s, there was an uncomfortable realization from within the movement itself that British Arts and Crafts were too narrowly focused. The rigorous rejection of mechanized production and the concomitant insistence on craft handwork invariably made their products economically exclusive. Within the constraints of the Arts and Crafts philosophy, William Morris who wanted 'an art by the people and for the people' had to admit that cheap art was impossible because 'all art costs time, trouble and thought'. Stylistically, there was also an ambiguity about Arts and Crafts simplicity. Romantic admiration for the vernacular, whether in architecture or the applied arts, and rationalist stripping down to essentials could achieve the same simplicity while at the same time obscuring the motives.

The Deutsche Werkbund, formed in 1907 in Germany, took the ideas of the Arts and Crafts movement a crucial stage further. It sought the improvement of the applied and decorative arts (and for the first time implicitly assumed that this included industrial products) through the combined and perforce equal efforts of industrialists, artists and craftsmen. This realignment of contributory forces inexorably moved the debate in favour of functionalism over ornamentation and laid the foundations of European Modernism, which has been the dominant aesthetic for the remainder of the century.

The moving spirit behind the Werkbund was Herman Muthesius (1861–1927), Superintendent of the Prussian Board of Trade for the Schools of Arts and

Crafts. Previously attached to the German embassy in London between 1896 and 1903 for research on English housing, he had been impressed by the work of the architects of the Arts and Crafts movement in achieving both reason and simplicity in building and art. Back in Germany, he began to proselytize these qualities as the virtues necessary to forge a new aesthetic for architecture and the applied arts. During a particularly notable speech in Berlin in 1907 he hectored manufacturers for continuing with 'the imitation of the hackneyed forms of bygone times'. Predictably (Muthesius was not shy of courting controversy), this aroused a storm of protest but had the intended result of attracting a number of adventurous architects, artists, writers and manufacturers to form the nucleus of the Werkbund. On another flank, acting in his official capacity, he appointed to art schools throughout Prussia teachers and principals who were willing to throw over sterile nineteenth-century orthodoxies and embrace the new principles of the Werkbund philosophy. This trend was repeated throughout Germany. The most notable appointments were the architect Peter Behrens, who became Principal of the Dusseldorf Academy of Art, and Henri van de Velde of the Weimar Art School.

The next significant stage in the development of the Modern Movement was the 1914 Werkbund exhibition in Cologne. This was distinguished, if not summed up by, the model factory designed by Walter Gropius and the glass house by Bruno Taut. Undoubtedly it would have been far more influential if it had not been abruptly closed by the outbreak of the First World War but it did inspire a group of English visitors from the Arts and Crafts Society to set up the Design and Industries Association (DIA) in direct imitation of and with the same objectives as the Deutsche Werkbund. The final, critical stage in establishing the new modernist aesthetic was the setting-up of the Bauhaus in 1919 under the direction of Walter Gropius. An architect by training and profession, Gropius saw architecture as a unifying force to which all other arts were subordinate. He extended the principles underlying the Werkbund to their logical conclusion, dictating that art and technology should be forged as a unity. Bauhaus teaching during its brief 14-year existence eliminated all decoration in architecture and the applied arts, reducing everything to its essentials: materials, functions and abstract relationships.

What effect, if any, did these developments have on European silver? Silverware manufacturers and designers had to be more conservative than their counterparts in the other decorative arts because of the cost of raw materials and of 'tooling up' for new designs and ornament was never entirely eschewed. Therefore an exclusively functionalist aesthetic was never a real possibility in silverware and did not emerge except through student experiments in the Bauhaus itself. One of the defining moments was the 1925 exhibition in Paris in which the strikingly geometric silver of Jean Puiforçat and Tétard Frères, discreetly embellished with rich materials providing subtle ornamentation that none the less underpinned the functional purpose of the design, made the most dramatic impact. The work of the Danish silversmith Christian Fjerdlingstad, who lived in Paris, was rather more subdued and yet showed a consistent and refined early form of Modernism. His fellow-national Georg Jensen showed an equally restrained form of Modernism that was to prove immensely popular, for his designs neatly and more obviously bridged the gap between European art nouveau, British Arts and Crafts and the new Modernism itself. The British contribution in 1925 was by contrast distinctly old-fashioned. The centrepiece of the display was Henry Wilson's standing cup surmounted by a figure of St George. This was strongly reminiscent of an Edwardian Arts and Crafts sumptuousness and exhibited little, if any, hint of the developments of the subsequent generation.

The British before the Second World War displayed a nervous regard for Modernism. The DIA did its best to promote the new aesthetic philosophy but the smallness of the organization, its voluntary and amateur nature and its ultimate reluctance to forego its Arts and Crafts origins limited its influence. Equally, the teaching in the art schools throughout the country was firmly entrenched in the Arts and Crafts. The Victoria and

Albert Museum for the first 50 years of the twentieth century had a policy of not acquiring contemporary silverware and so played little part in promoting modern design in this sphere. The London Goldsmiths' Company, however, pursued an enlightened policy from 1925 of acquiring a collection of modern British silver and promoting it wherever possible through a series of exhibitions and trade fairs. The most notable were the Dorland House exhibition of 1933, the Royal Academy exhibition of 1935 and the 1938 exhibition of modern British silver at Goldsmiths' Hall. If it had not been for the consistent and dedicated efforts of the Goldsmiths' Company in conjunction with informal advice from the Design and Industries Association, British silverware would have been infinitely poorer.

Keith Murray trained as an architect and was the consultant designer to Mappin & Webb in the 1930s.

THE POST-WAR REVIVAL

The industrial reconstruction that was so necessary in Europe after the Second World War provided the opportunity for increasing integration of the crafts and industrial practice. Throughout Europe in the two decades that followed the war, silversmiths were encouraged not only to practise their craft but also to engage in design for manufacturing industry.

In Britain, this diversification was specifically promoted by the teaching offered at the Royal College of Art (RCA). In 1948 the RCA was on the brink of closure since for much of the century it had singularly failed in the task for which it had originally been established: to provide adequately trained designers for industry. In 1934 the Design and Industries Association had published a trenchant memorandum that stated: 'Art education is at present characterized by a bias towards the fine arts and a divorce from industry which is equally a divorce from the needs of our time...There is no provision for adequate instruction in industrial design...The Royal College of Art was founded for this purpose but its teaching has been deflected towards the fine arts and the training of art teachers.'

The RCA was reprieved by the Ministry of Education which decided to act on a report it had commissioned from the fledgling Council of Industrial Design. This report, never published, was none the less an impressive document. Written with consistent logic and common sense, it deprecated the traditional division in British education between the arts and the sciences, the art schools and the technical schools, and the schools of commerce and the universities. It paid particular attention to the RCA about which Robin Darwin, who wrote the report, commented: 'Much would, of course,

depend upon the Principal, and the initial appointment would be a factor of pivotal importance for the ultimate development of the school.' This proved to be a prescient statement for it was Darwin himself who was appointed as Principal two years later. In many respects he was an inspired choice. Darwin insisted on (and was granted) full academic freedom, thus initiating an era of intellectual stimulation and exchange that had hitherto eluded the institution. He reorganized the departmental structure so that the College conformed more closely to industrial disciplines and recruited the best talent available for his teaching staff. Robert Goodden, who had trained and worked as an architect, craftsman and designer, was appointed as Head of the School of Silversmithing and Jewellery. Goodden's achievement was to establish a course that equally served the needs of mass-production metalwork industries and the craft of silversmithing.

The effect of these reforms was startling and immediate. Three of the most eminent British silversmiths of the later part of the twentieth century graduated from the RCA in the mid-1950s: Gerald Benney, Robert Welch and David Mellor. Shortly after graduation, all three were offered design consultancies with large manufacturing tableware firms in the Midlands: Benney with Viners, Welch with Old Hall and Mellor with Walker & Hall. Several Design Council Awards followed.

However, this work was not undertaken at the expense of their attention to silversmithing nor were their industrial consultancies the sole means of subsidizing the craft. Here the Goldsmiths' Company again played an important role. The Company gave support

In this service Robert Goodden's design is combined with Leslie Durbin's chasing and engraving.

to such major exhibitions as 'Britain Can Make It', held at the Victoria and Albert Museum in 1948, by organizing a competition and arranging the silver exhibit from the Hall. During the Festival of Britain in 1951 it staged an exhibition of contemporary plate at the Hall to show that the craft was alive and flourishing. Such overt promotion in international exhibitions, both at home and abroad, has continued ever since. For this the credit is largely due to Graham Hughes, Art Director between 1945 and 1981, who furthermore offered practical help to young graduates by facilitating commissions, sometimes from the Hall itself for its own collection. Benney, Welch and Mellor directly benefited from this initiative as well as subsequent RCA graduates such as Alex Styles, Keith Redfern, Stuart Devlin and Eric Clements.

The period 1945–65 can rightly be regarded as the heroic age of Modernism in British silver. Collectively,

the work is distinguished by a formal geometry, relatively unembellished and with purity of line. The Scandinavian influence, particularly in the 1950s, is clear. Henning Koppel's designs for the Danish firm of Georg Jensen use expressive, sweeping curves that give his objects a monumental grandeur and sculptural quality, and tease the philosophy of functionalism to its limits. The slightly attenuated forms of Benney's early work reflect these developments and Robert Welch has always openly acknowledged his debt to the work of the Swedish silversmith Sigurd Persson. Persson's thematic, thorough treatment of silver hollow-ware and jewellery shows a clarity and control that despite certain organic details, such as the swan-like necks of his coffee pots, provides a series of definitive, abstract statements of lasting international influence.

Benney's mature style displays a more formal and symmetrical element which is often enriched by

77

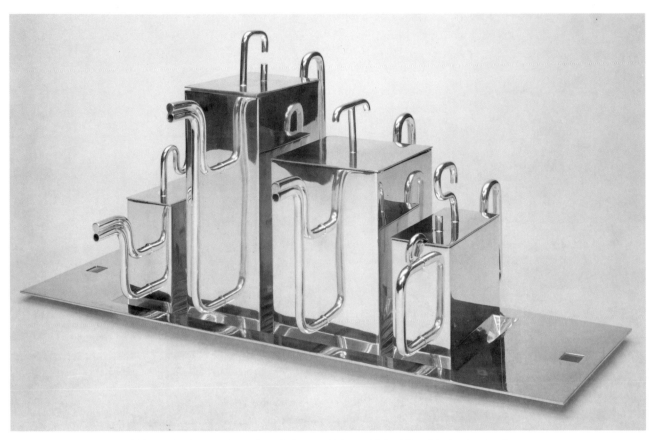

This service is one of a series of eleven which established Post Modernism in silver.

textured surfaces and the use of deep lustrous enamel. Benney has always succeeded in keeping his embellishment tightly disciplined although even the heroic modernists began to introduce picturesque and ornamental factors into their work. The younger generation of British silversmiths in the past two decades introduce an overt decorative quality. Rod Kelly, who is rapidly establishing himself as one of the foremost chasers in Britain, uses his skills to form an illustrated surface to his objects, usually referring in a literal way to the circumstances of the commission to hand. Kevin Coates and Lexi Dick, who started their careers as jewellers, increasingly use three-dimensional figure-modelling to describe the object's function. Coates also experiments with a rich range of colours. Colour is enjoying a revival through the art of enamelling and, apart from Coates, Jane Short and Fred Rich are proving to be very accomplished practitioners (see 'International Highlights').

The economic recessions of the 1970s and '80s permanently altered European manufacturing industry and swept away the optimism of the 1950s and '60s. Then, design was about changing society. By the 1980s it was associated merely with marketing and 'lifestyle'. No longer could silversmiths subsidize their craft by design consultancies and nor could they claim that they were part of the mainstream culture. The individual silversmith returned to operating in a niche market and, in some respects, this has had a curiously liberating effect. In Europe since the 1970s increasing attention has been given to the individual quality of the craftsmanship and less emphasis has been placed on a unified aesthetic philosophy. The range of work has become more diverse. The Post-Modern experiments in Italy during the 1980s redefined the public perception of Modernism itself. The Alessi company of Milan commissioned a group of international architects to design a collection of tea and coffee services; the series of startling tableaux that were produced excited world attention. These services were barely functional; some incorporated obvious historical references and all show a degree of deconstruction, an architectural and sculptural movement that surfaced during the 1980s. The commissioning of architects to design silver is by no means novel but has been very successfully used by the Italians to inject a stimulating freshness and vitality into contemporary silverware design, whether the flamboyant experiments of Alessi and Cleto Munari or the more sober, classic approach of the San Lorenzo studio.

Australia is starting to establish an indigenous silversmithing tradition. Two Europeans, Johannes Kuhnen from Germany and Ragnar Hansen from Norway, now run the postgraduate silversmithing and jewellery course at the Canberra School of Art where they have initiated a range of challenging experiments that combine traditional and new materials. They and their students have gained international recognition and their work is beginning to feed back into the European mainstream. During the second half of the 20th century, the craft of silversmithing has certainly retrenched but, considering the new developments that are happening in a global context, there is every reason to feel confident about and have faith in its future.

Sigurd Persson has enjoyed an internationally successful career as a silversmith, jeweller and industrial designer.

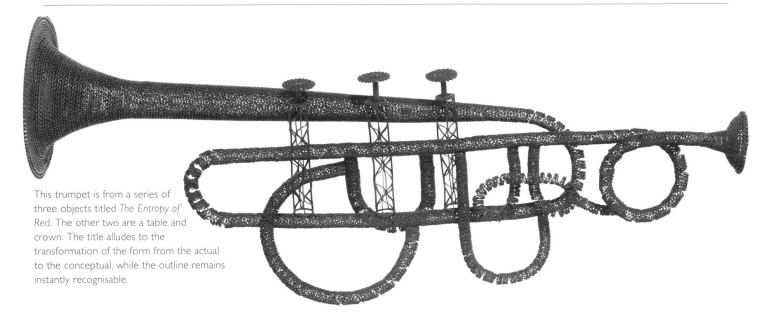

This trumpet is from a series of three objects titled *The Entropy of Red*. The other two are a table and crown. The title alludes to the transformation of the form from the actual to the conceptual, while the outline remains instantly recognisable.

An extraordinary diversity in silver is evident at the end of the 20th century although Modernism is the classic style of this period, as the work of the Milan studio San Lorenzo convincingly demonstrates. San Lorenzo was established in 1970 with the intention of creating a new idiom in silver. Since then it has established an impressive range of products, each offering a complete reappraisal of the conventional function and appearance and all designed by architects with significant national and international reputations. Architects have also contributed significantly to mainstream silver design, particularly in Italy.

Elsewhere, there has been increasing exploration of the subtleties of technique, as with Yukie Osumi (b. 1945) whose work is among the finest to be produced in Japan today. It is characterized by gracefully proportioned forms and generously flowing surface patterning. In Australia Johannes Kuhnen and Robert Foster conduct interesting experiments incorporating new materials in fascinating combinations. Kuhnen (b. 1952) studied under Frederich Becker and Sigrid Delius in his native Germany before moving to Australia in 1981. His work reflects the cool precision of modern German practice, in which simple geometric forms are combined with technical innovation.

Colour, whether introduced by the use of such materials or more traditionally by the use of enamel is making a welcome comeback, as in the work of Fred Rich and Jane Short in Britain. Fred Rich (b.1954) is noted for his rich enamel work, often set with precious and semi-precious gemstones, which has a strong representational quality. Rich, who works as both jeweller and silversmith, is one of the younger generation that is rapidly establishing a significant reputation. The work of the British silversmith Michael Rowe explores the geometric formalism of Modernism, subject to the apparent distortions of individual perception. His work is increasingly academic and unconcerned with function. As in the 1920s, the exchange between jewellery and silversmithing has led to a growth in decorative silver that at times is clearly anti-modernistic. The Australian Robert Baines discards the functionalism so characteristic of 20th-century metalwork and instead explores the spiritual significance of the goldsmiths' craft to produce silverwork and jewellery of ritual and totemic significance. The future is bright.

The work of Fred Rich has gained maturity and assurance over recent years. His training as a jeweller has given him a technical virtuosity clearly evident in this salt produced for Garrards in 1995. The technique of cloisonné enamel has been used to give a vivid pictorial quality and polychromatic effect to the surface of the metal.

In the technique employed by Yukie Osumi for this vase, metal leaf and wire are hammered into a fine mesh-like grid and then incised into the surface of the metal ground. The vase, called Heat Haze, has also been pickled and polished to give the very subtle range of colours that is a distinctive feature of Osumi's maturing style.

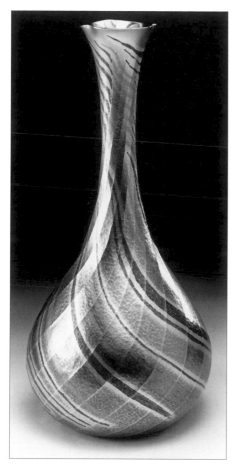

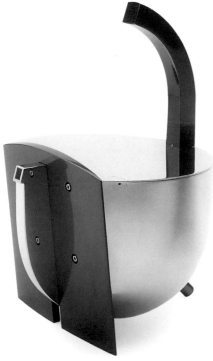

This teapot incorporates all the salient characteristics of Johannes Kuhnen's current work. Following a well-established 20th-century German tradition, he explores basic geometric forms, bisecting them with vivid sections of colour. He is responsible for introducing anodising, and a degree of technical finish which has prompted new departures in Australian metalwork.

The architectural partnership of Afra and Tobia Scarpa has created many of the most successful designs produced by the San Lorenzo studio over the past twenty-five years. The form of these vessels is the result of a thorough re-evaluation of the object's functional aspect. The textured surfaces are created by the silversmith applying a variety of punches at his own discretion.

—II—

THE CRAFT

The elaborate late Baroque vase flourished by Crespin was admired for its design and workmanship.

WHAT IS A GOLDSMITH?

The Goldsmith ought to be a good designer and have good Taste in Sculpture. He must be conversant in Alchemy: that is in all the Properties of metals...He must know the various Ways of Essaying Metals, and distinguishing the real from the fictitious...he ought to be possessed of a solid Judgement as well as a mechanical Hand and Head. Designing is the chief Part of his early Study, previous to his Apprenticeship.

R. CAMPBELL, *THE LONDON TRADESMAN*, 1747

Both in French and in English, the terminology for the craft has always stressed gold, the nobler metal. Guilds of goldsmiths encompassed all those concerned with the precious metals, although silversmiths were always far more numerous than workers in gold. From the humble and anonymous burnisher (who was often a woman) to the goldsmith–banker, a wide spectrum of skills and wealth was encompassed within the goldsmiths' craft. The records of English and continental craft guilds name those admitted to the status of master, those entering a formal apprenticeship, foreigners licensed to work and those caught out in misdemeanours. They ignore the shadowy mass of journeymen and those in related but peripheral crafts such as spangle- or buckle-making, refining, gold-beating or wire-drawing. Anything to do with the precious metals touched the goldsmiths' craft in some way or another. Hundreds were employed or self-employed in large centres such as Paris or London although the coveted title of 'citizen and goldsmith' was confined to a small number.

An apprentice's engraving of his father's shop and workshop, 1646.

Qualifications for access to the goldsmiths' craft varied from city to city and were lighter for the sons of natives. When an apprentice, almost always a boy, finished his indentured term of between four and seven years, he expected to work as a journeyman to gain experience and accumulate patterns and sketches. The German and Flemish cities required journeymen to travel for a period called the *Wanderjahre* (three years for Zurich journeymen), to obtain fresh ideas. A few (numbers were usually restricted to protect the interests of the craft) then attained the status of master and the right to run a shop. In Paris from 1571 the goldsmiths' guild determined that there were to be only 300 serving a population of more than 100,000. In the mid-seventeenth century the guilds in both Paris and London each had a membership of about 450. Access to the guild was through the making of a masterpiece, often under examination conditions. The aspiring

WITHOWT. THE. BLESINGE.
GOD. LABOVR. IS.
NOTHYNG :

· ÆTATIS · SVÆ · 40
·; 1565 :·

John Lonyson became Second Warden of the Goldsmiths'
Company, to whom he bequeathed a gilt ewer and basin.

master chose whether to prove his skill by devising, raising and decorating something large, such as a cup or salt, or by making a jewel or ring and setting it with a stone. In Augsburg, for example, a goldsmith had to work under the eye of one of the wardens and his piece was locked away at night for the six weeks that was allowed for its completion. In London the Goldsmiths' Company failed to enforce consistently the requirement for the masterpiece, despite recurrent criticisms in the sixteenth and seventeenth centuries of the low standard of English workmanship. Their superior skills gave the better-trained Flemish, German or French craftsmen who made up nearly a tenth of the working community of the London craft a distinct advantage.

The essential starting-point for success as a goldsmith was, as the Paris regulations stated, to be 'de bon nom et de bonne fame', in other words to be of legiti-

mate birth to a settled family with a good reputation. Apprentices carried part-finished work to and from the assay office, they took pieces to the engraver or chaser and they had to be reliable. Daily access to precious metals offered great temptations for dishonesty or discreditable behaviour. A close family network linked members of the craft and they often lived and worked in close proximity. Tudor Cheapside was famous for its Goldsmiths' Row where the principal masters lived and sold their wares. When the retailers moved westwards to the Haymarket and Lincoln's Inn Fields from the late seventeenth century, the workshops followed, clustering in the smaller streets in Clerkenwell and Soho nearby.

The distinctions between a goldsmith, a silversmith and a plateworker were both economic and social. John Lonyson (d.1582) son of a Brabant goldsmith who had settled in King's Lynn, became a master worker at the Tower Mint. The coat of arms, his sober but costly black garment and the very act of commissioning a portrait mark him out as a prominent and prosperous Londoner with a shop and house in Goldsmiths' Row, Cheapside. Dress codes dictated a hat and gloves for a master goldsmith, as in the mid-seventeenth century French engraving of a workshop, whereas journeymen wore aprons and caps with flaps. Secure in their status as creative artists and master goldsmiths supplying the aristocracy, the Huguenot Paul Crespin and his contemporary Thomas Germain in Paris chose to have themselves depicted in working attire and with highly worked plate. Successful English goldsmiths preferred to be portrayed as gentlemen in ruffles, lace and velvet. His diary shows that Samuel Pepys dealt with wealthy goldsmith–bankers such as Edward Backwell or Thomas Vyner, entrepreneurs who had little to do with the day-to-day production of plate. Pepys also bought domestic plate and had it cleaned and repaired by various retailers – Stephens, Stokes, Colvill, Pinckney – men who would take old plate or 'Burnt or Unburnt Lace' in payment. Workshops were run by a third, smaller group which included the composer Wallington, 'a poor working goldsmith that goes without gloves to his hands'. Engravers and chasers, the most highly paid craftsmen, were independent and self-employed, working at piece-rates, often in garrets and back rooms away from the more expensive street-side properties.

From the seventeenth century at least, members of the London Goldsmiths' Company were prominent in all kinds of business and some goldsmiths were free, that is members of other companies. Through his father Paul Storr was free of the Vintners' Company and Thomas Jenkins, the late Stuart retailer, was a Butcher. Alien goldsmiths working under royal favour, such as Christian van Vianen, brought from Utrecht by Charles I, or Benvenuto Cellini in Renaissance Paris, were never made free of the local craft and could not mark their wares under their own names. More modest stranger goldsmiths bringing letters of introduction could obtain licences to work. A complaint in 1621 to the Privy Council from the Goldsmiths' Company lists 179 aliens and strangers who 'do take away a great part of the living and maintenance of the free goldsmiths of this city', but those same skilled foreign jewellers, stone-cutters, enamellers, engravers and chasers supplied the court with costly luxuries. The wardens of the Company, as businessmen, had to consider where their best interests lay. So, although the stream of complaints from the Society of Working Goldsmiths flowed on until the mid-eighteenth century, the Company had an ambivalent attitude to foreign plate. Matthew Boulton attempted at his Soho Manufactory in the 1770s to break away from the traditional apprenticeship system, employing local boys and girls and setting up an embryonic production line with the intention of cutting costs. Although his highly crafted large plate was not as successful as he hoped (the London businesses had easier access to all the various skills needed, see 'A London Business'), his methods were effective for the Sheffield plate side of the business where hand-finishing was not essential.

Attitudes to women in shops and workshop varied from time to time and from place to place. In many English towns, and probably in most of northern Europe, daughters, wives and sisters worked as junior partners, keeping accounts, supervising shops or carrying out specific finishing tasks such as burnishing.

Virtually invisible to the official record until they were widowed, many then ran businesses, registered marks, took apprentices and sometimes ended up marrying the workshop manager, as the Londoner Rebecca Emes, widow of John Emes, did in 1808. Her successful partnership with Edward Barnard ran almost until her death in 1829. Barnard's was to become the largest manufacturing business in London with a thriving export trade, especially to India. However, the role of most women was limited to home-working on small wares such as buttons, spectacles or spoons, or burnishing.

The responsibility of the guild for collecting royal exactions (dues, duties, taxes, forced loans) and for the misdeeds of its members was always a fear and a spur to the wardens, who sought out and punished makers and sellers of substandard wares. But they were policing the standard of the alloy, not the quality of the manufacture. The London Company asserted its right to carry out searches and seize substandard objects in provincial towns and at regional fairs until the mid-eighteenth century. But by this time production was beginning in new unregulated centres such as Birmingham and Sheffield and the long-standing institutional monopolies had effectively dissolved. The corporate life of the London, Newcastle, Chester and Exeter companies became increasingly inward-looking and the London Company was revitalized only in the mid-nineteenth century.

Women burnishers finishing plate in the Christofle factory, about 1860.

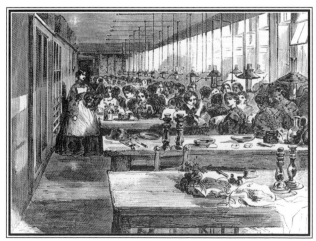

The assay warden striking a mark.

Goldsmiths led a rich corporate life, clubbing together to acquire halls for business and hospitality. This chest belonging to the Ulm Goldsmiths' Guild is painted with the heraldic devices and merchant marks of the members from 1500. They flank a painting of St Eligius, the patron saint of the Guild, in a workshop.

Marks struck into silver are the oldest form of consumer protection. They indicate the place of making, the standard of purity, the official who tested that standard and the master responsible for the piece. They can also record that tax has been paid, as in the English duty mark of a monarch's head (1784–1890), or the French *charge* and *décharge* marks introduced in 1677. Goldsmiths dealt in the raw material of the currency and a close link has always existed between a precious metal coinage and the manufacture of gold and silver wares.

The earliest continuous marking system dates from 500 AD in the reign of the Byzantine Emperor Anastasius, but the origins of the European marks lie in the thirteenth century. From the late Anglo-Saxon period craft and trade associations, known as guilds or mysteries, emerged in towns for mutual support, to control price and standard and to exclude outsiders. These guilds acquired property in the form of the halls in which they ate, drank and worshipped together and were tightly controlled by the civic authorities and by royal decree. To load on to the corporation of goldsmiths the responsibility for controlling, testing and marking plate was an obvious step, particularly since the tightly knit senior membership was likely to include Mint and other royal officers responsible for the currency and the supply of bullion.

In Paris a royal mark was already in use when the king's mark of *une teste de leone* was stipulated for English plate in 1300. The guarantee offered by hallmarks made a real difference to the sale price of plate. The official standard of purity of the alloy varied from one city to another and in some frontier regions, especially in the south of the Netherlands, more than one standard was recognized. Steel punches were used to make the hallmarks. Some were small enough to mark inside a gold ring, watchcase or snuffbox.

Right: This markplate from Ghent is engraved with the names and struck with the marks of 108 goldsmiths. The London Goldsmiths' Company had changed to paper records in 1697 after two disastrous fires had destroyed the Assay Office.

Far right: The mark of the goldsmith could identify the workshop responsible for making the object, a subcontractor assembling a large order or a retailer. From the 1850s the mark was believed to identify the maker. Only in the past 25 years has this convenient assumption been unpicked and the true complexity of the network of suppliers and retailers acknowledged. About 1608 the London Assay Office introduced part-marking for hinges, handles, lids and other components.

Above: Signature of Charles Kandler (b. 1695), elder brother of the Meissen modeller J.J. Kaëndler, in the Largeworkers' Book at the Goldsmiths' Hall. Punches were dipped in lampblack (soot) to create an official record. Kandler registered several more marks and was joined by his younger brother Frederick after 1739.

Bottom right: The mark of the fashionable Huguenot goldsmith Elizabeth Godfrey (EG in a lozenge) is struck over and partly conceals the mark of her supplier who made this caster in 1754–55. Daughter of a goldsmith and twice widowed, she ran a shop off the Haymarket.

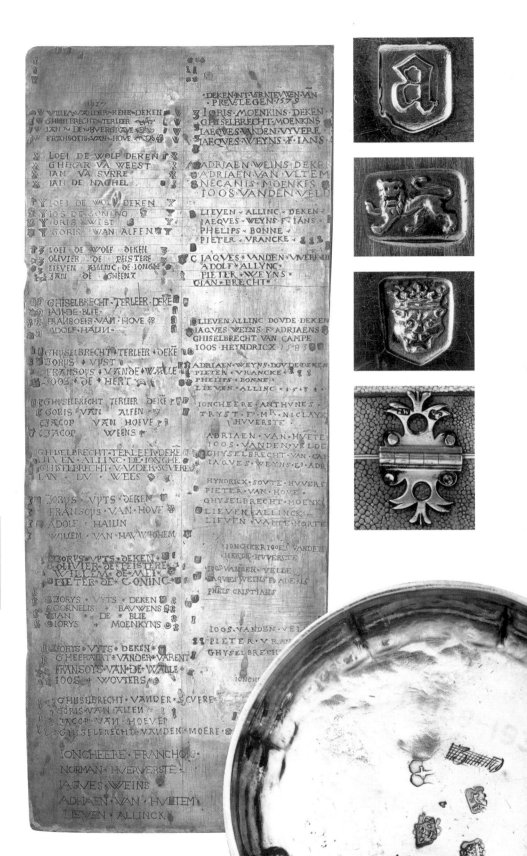

WORKING AND DECORATING SILVER

Raising a bowl on a stake by using a hammer.

Raising

This technique enables a hollow shape to be produced from a flat disc of silver. The disc is held over a rounded metal stake or anvil and worked with a hammer in a concentric pattern to turn it into a rounded form. The contours of the stake and the type of hammer are varied according to the desired form or shape. When producing a shallow dished shape, an alternative preliminary technique known as blocking is used to hammer a flat sheet of silver into a hollowed-out profile in a block. Hammering metal hardens it and makes it difficult to work. By the process of frequent annealing, in which the silver is heated to a dull red then quenched in water, silver is prevented from cracking while it is worked.

Embossing

In the decorative technique known as embossing or repoussé work, the design is produced from the reverse without removing any metal. The piece to be worked is placed face down on a block made of a resilient material such as lead, wood or pitch. The design is then pricked on to the back and worked using punches and a light hammer. The supporting block must be resilient enough to allow the silver to be impressed by the punches, but offer sufficient resistance to prevent the indentation from being too deep. The head of the punch can be various shapes or engraved with a design. Repeated hammering with the simple rounded shape known as an embosser produces broader, repeating patterns. Embossing is often followed by and combined with chasing to create a subtle effect and higher relief decoration.

Chasing

Chasing is another technique that enables silver to be decorated without removing any metal. The design is pricked on to the surface of the object, sometimes using a stencil or following a three-dimensional pattern in lead, or plaster by eye. The object is then placed on a specially prepared bed of pitch combined with plaster of Paris and resin, or filled with pitch. The pitch mixture provides a firm working surface that is also resilient and can be melted and removed once the chasing has been completed. A light chasing-hammer is used with punches to produce a decorative effect by pushing the silver into relief. Flat-chasing, in which the design is worked on to the flat surface, can easily be identified as it leaves an image of the punched design on the reverse. The punches are held at an angle with the top furthest from the silversmith so that the progress of the chased design can be monitored.

An iron plaque embossed and damascened in gold and silver. Milan, about 1550.

Engraving

A design can be cut into the surface of silver with a steel cutting-tool that removes a thin sliver of metal, called a burin or graver. Gravers are short with wooden handles that fit the palm of the hand. A professional engraver will have a large number of gravers, each suited to a particular engraving task. The work is held firm on the engraver's block, which is basically a weighted ball with an adjustable clamp. Bright-cutting is a form of engraving in which the metal is cut at an angle to create facets which reflect the light.

Etching

Surface decoration can also be produced by etching with acid. Two methods are commonly used. In relief etching an acid-resisting material is painted on the surface in the required design. When the object is placed in a bath of acid the unprotected areas are eaten away leaving the design in relief. For the alternative method of intaglio etching the entire surface of the object is covered with acid-resistant and the design is then scored through the thickness of the material to the metal. The acid is then used to cut away the exposed areas.

The most commonly used acid-resistant, asphaltum varnish, can be painted on to a metal surface with a brush. Hydrochloric and nitric acids in various solutions and combinations are those generally used in the

This plaque, embossed and chased with a scene of Christ with the woman of Samaria, is signed by
Christopher Heckel and dated 1772.

etching process. The depth of the etching depends on the strength of the acid and the length of time the object remains in the bath. Etching is more commonly used on iron and steel than on gold or silver wares.

Colouring

Gold and silver wares can be coloured by using chemicals and heat treatments. Silver for example can be turned black by treating the surface with a solution of sulphur, ammonia and water. Low-carat gold can be turned to a copper colour by subjecting it to slow heat. The traditional method of gilding, a widely used colouring process for silver, was known as mercury or amalgam gilding. This was made illegal in England in the 1920s as the process was extremely toxic. Red-hot plates of gold were placed in an iron ladle filled with boiling mercury where they combined to form an amal-

gam. The amalgam was put into a bag of chamois leather and the surplus mercury squeezed out until it had the consistency of thick paste. The object to be gilded was thoroughly cleaned and heated before the gold–mercury amalgam was painted on with a brush. The object was then placed over a fire or in an oven and brought to a low red heat to drive off the mercury in the form of vapour. The remaining gold adhered to the surface, which was then polished and burnished. Since the development of electrodeposition in the nineteenth century, gilding on metal has almost invariably been done by electroplating.

Enamelling

Colour has been applied to gold and silver wares by enamelling from early times. Enamel is created by heating up the materials from which glass is made –

flint or sand, red lead and potash or soda. Colour is produced by adding a metallic oxide, such as copper for green and cobalt for blue. The mixture is then ground into powder, placed on a prepared surface and fired in an oven to make it adhere. Widely used in the medieval period to decorate gold and silver as on the Mérode Cup (see 'The Middle Ages'), the art was revived in the nineteenth century by designers such as A.W.N. Pugin. Contemporary enamellers include Jane Short and Fred Rich.

Niello

The decorative treatment called niello is particularly employed in Eastern Europe and the Baltic countries. The design is either etched or engraved into the surface of the silver. A powdered or granular mixture consisting of the sulphides of silver, copper and lead is pushed into the etched or engraved lines and fused by heat. The surface is then polished. Niello has a distinctive lustrous black colour which provides a vivid contrast with the bright surface of silver.

Damascening

Gold and silver were frequently used to decorate base metals, especially bronze and iron. Precious metals can be soldered directly on to a surface, a technique known as overlay, or inlaid, which is known as damascening. There are two forms of this technique, which was used especially on iron. The first and most common is known as false damascening. The iron object was first heated and blued. The surface was then deeply cross-hatched with a knife or broad chisel before, using a brass point so that it would show up clearly, the design was drawn on it. Very pure and soft gold or silver wire was forced into the notches cut into the surface of the iron by tapping with a hammer and punch. False damascening can be recognized by the finely hatched lines that appear next to the areas of the design. For true damascening, the pattern was cut directly into the surface using an engraving tool or chisel that left a 'dove-tail' channel. A hammer and punch were used to force the gold or silver wire into the channel. The dove-tail section held the wire very firmly, hence this form of inlay was very durable. However, since the cutting of the design required the skill of an engraver and more wire was used in this technique, it took longer and was therefore more expensive.

These 1690s dessert stands have chased borders, engraved heraldry and cast rims and feet.

The starting point for the silversmith was a silver ingot or bar, until the mid-eighteenth century when the technique of rolling sheet was adopted. The man to the left is pouring molten silver into a mould.

Casting is a method of shaping metal and making copies. In its simplest form, a silver ingot (which itself is cast as the final stage of the refining process) is melted in a crucible, then poured into a mould and left to solidify. Any material that is hard and heat-resistant can be used to make a mould. Bronze and fine-grained stone were the most common substances although silver wares were usually cast in sand. The making of the initial pattern requires very great skill as it determines the final design. An initial model is made in wax or clay and then copied in a more permanent form in lead, brass, wood or plaster. This pattern is then pressed into sand. Casting has been and continues to be used by silversmiths to make buttons, knife hafts and spoon finials as well as such components of larger wares as feet for tureens, handles for ewers and borders for salvers. Cast elements are often produced in multiples. This method has also been used to produce applied motifs which are then soldered on after surfaces have been filed smooth. Silver soldering relies on

the capillary action between close-fitting surfaces and when skilfully done the solder line becomes invisible. Modern silversmiths are making increasing use of centrifuged casting where the metal is forced into the mould using centrifugal force. This permits work of the finest detail to be reproduced repeatedly.

This bronze two-part mould for casting a small devotional statue in solid silver has locating pins and holes. It was clamped tightly together at the cut-away sides before the molten silver was poured through the hole under the Virgin's feet.

Left: The candlestick base on the left, made in London in 1693, has been raised from sheet and the bands of gadroons created by stamping. A separate strip has then been soldered around the foot. The base on the right, also made in London, has been cast in one piece, with a hole left for a separately cast stem. Although the cast candlestick cost more initially because a casting pattern had to be made, numerous copies could be produced. It used more silver than the raised method but the extra cost could be passed on to the purchaser.

Below: Between 1720 and 1760 many small fancy objects such as cream jugs incorporating fashionable high-relief ornament were made by casting. The body of this jug was cast with its swirls and inset scenes in two halves and the handle and foot separately. The chaser then worked the surface to conceal the joins. The seam is visible inside the jug, running from lip to handle. The thickness of the metal and the lack of work on the interior demonstrate that this piece is cast. A casting was sometimes chased up and extra details added.

This ewer from a toilet service makes lavish use of several casting patterns, which have been combined and applied with great skill. The foot and knop incorporating gadroons, the ribs cradling the base, the shells and arches and the gadrooned girdle with the helmeted mask are all standard components. The richly modelled figure handle was cast in at least two parts and a vertical seam is visible despite subsequent chasing. Fine casting using 'Paris sand' was a French speciality.

Silver has always been admired for the soft lustrous sheen it has when it is burnished and polished to a high degree of reflectivity. However, the surface of silver tarnishes or blackens in the atmosphere when it comes into contact with sulphur. Peas, eggs and Brussels sprouts all contain sulphur and so trigger this reaction and chemicals like ammonia, ozone and hydrogen sulphide attack silver in a different way. Airborne pollution from heavy traffic and fumes from burning oil and gas contribute to tarnishing, especially in cities. Until the mid-19th century keeping silver clean and polished was time-consuming, messy and laborious. Domestic cleaning demanded damaging abrasives: 'Rub the flagons and chalices from the top to the Bottom not crosswise but the Bason and patens are to be rubbed roundwise not across and by no means use either chalk, sand or salt' were the instructions for cleaning Carlisle Cathedral plate, 1680. Clients could return plate to the goldsmith for 'boiling and burnishing' that is, a bath in acid to remove stains. In 1839 the chemist Joseph Goddard developed the first commercial silver polish, his Non-Mercurial Plate Polish, and his company has continued to evolve cleaning materials and tarnish-inhibitors ever since.

When candlelight was replaced first by oil and gas and then by electric light in the late 19th century, silver in the dining room was expected to shine with a new brilliance. Commercial finishes on both silver and electroplate were dazzling. But by 1851 aesthetes and connoisseurs felt a growing discomfort with this crude 'Birmingham-bright' look and the 'flashiness' of English silver. Experiments with colouring, frosting, oxidization and other surface treatments flourished. Old silver was allowed to oxidize slightly and patina, the build-up

Above: The conservator is chemically removing heavy tarnish from an early 18th-century cooler with swabs of Silver Dip and rinsing it with de-ionized water to remove all chemical residues. Because the cooler is too large for the fume cupboard to be effective, a mask is worn to protect the conservator from hydrogen sulphide.

Below: Jonathan Swift's *Directions to Servants*, 1745

of myriad small scratches from wear, was admired and valued. When the firm Elkington's went to Russia in the 1880s to make electrotype copies of the old English silver in the Kremlin and the Hermitage, they met a long-standing tradition of not cleaning historic silver. This conservative attitude continued until very recently and has resulted in good preservation of the surface details. Lord Rosebery at Mentmore displayed his antique silver 'so tarnished that it resembled pewter. This was not due to any lack of care or an underestimation of its value... but had for many years been customary with continental collections to prevent the silver from over-zealous polishing in the butler's pantry.'

To the Butler:
When you clean your Plate, leave the Whiting plainly to be seen in all the chinks for fear your lady should not believe you had cleaned it.

To the Cook:
If you have a silver Saucepan for the kitchen use, let me advise you to batter it well and keep it always black; this will be for your masters honour, for it shews there has been constant good housekeeping: And make room for the Saucepan by wriggling it on the coals.
In the same manner, if you are allowed a large silver spoon for the Kitchen, let half the Bole of it be worn out with continual stirring and scraping and often say merrily, 'This Spoon owes my Master no Service'.

This large Elizabethan salt was photographed shortly after it was purchased by the V&A in 1888. It had been stored in a bank for many years and was allowed to retain its darkened surface until the 1920s.
The details of chasing and punching show up here more clearly than in a later photograph.

Diffusion samplers are used to measure levels of pollutants in a silver store. The pollutants include hydrogen sulphide, nitrogen dioxide, sulphur dioxide and volatile organic compounds such as acetic acid given off by wooden cases. The investigation will inform the design of new storage and display units in the V&A.

The Islington Cup, made as a presentation piece in 1802, has been stored in its lined case and rarely handled. Its original contrasting surfaces, part gilded and burnished, part matt, part white, chased and textured, are unusually well preserved. It now has a removable coat of lacquer to protect the metal from the atmosphere, as do virtually all the silver objects in the V&A.

DESIGN

The ability to draw was essential for goldsmiths. Here a master sketches in the corner of his shop.

L et nothing be omitted, either in the curiousness of the workmanship or quality of the pieces that may add either grace or beauty unto them

JAMES I'S DIRECTIONS FOR NEW PLATE, 1604

However skilled the silversmith and however well-equipped the workshop, it was the initial concept that determined the aesthetic quality of the object. Although the starting-point for a design could originate with heraldry, as in the Sprimont tureen, or with personal whim, like the revival of late fifteenth-century chalices by Bishop Lancelot Andrewes for altar plate in the 1620s and '30s, most designs for silver drew on the visual vocabulary current in other media. Strapwork, acanthus and 'c' scrolls were taken into the workshop and reproduced by artisans through a little-documented sequence of transmutation. Drawing was the key skill in this process, combined with the ability to envisage and work up an object in the round from a flat sheet of paper and translate a pencil line into the substantial weight of ingot or sheet required. Silver has always been a key indicator of taste and standing and people have always admired and sought new designs, even if they cost more.

Goldsmiths found that travel offered a key to 'invention' and inspiration, particularly during the *Wanderjahre*, the period of travel customary for northern European (although not English) journeymen from the fifteenth to the late eighteenth century. The Zurich goldsmith Hans Peter Oeri travelled between 1657 and 1663 in Germany and Italy 'and came home charged with art treasures', including recognizably French copper models. Augsburg was unusual in tolerating Protestant and Roman Catholic workmen, and this openness to influences from abroad was a significant factor in its pre-eminence.

Most of the collections of models and designs on paper that were so essential for goldsmiths have been dispersed. The Historical Museum in Basle preserves the workshop collection of Jorg Schweiger (c.1470–1553), who was closely linked to the Holbein family. This exemplifies the goldsmith's need for diverse sources: late Gothic models sit beside the latest 1560s strapwork casting patterns and several hundred sheets of ornament. The plaquettes devised by Peter Flötner (c.1484–1546) for casting Classical subjects were copied and rapidly reached London, for example a salt is listed in Henry VIII's collection and there are two salts in the Vintners' Company and the Tower of London.

An artist's palette, chasing tools, a globe cup and mathematical instruments are showered on the artist–goldsmith, Christopher Jamnitzer.

A strikingly eclectic mixture of styles and periods was inevitably to be found in the pattern rooms in any large nineteenth- or twentieth-century manufacturing business. When Beatrix Potter visited the premises of Hunt & Roskell in London in 1881 she was shown the room with screw presses for making handles and spouts about which she commented: 'One side was divided off into pigeon holes in which were kept innumerable steel dies. They were beautifully cut and worth several thousand pound…In the room beyond, small twirls chiefly belonging to candelabras were cast…The walls were hung with plaster casts…in a room leading out of the studio, all the designs were kept, over seven thousand.' The London manufacturers Vanders in Hatton Garden and Comyn's (recently re-established in Malaysia) boast large collections of dies, patterns, moulds and designs, many of which have been in use for more than a century.

A set of designs could be copied, reprinted and plundered for ideas over many years. Stefano della Bella (1610–64) was born in Florence but travelled between Paris and Rome, publishing more than 1,400 etchings. His friezes of foliage, dogs and putti were exploited and adapted in London, Paris, Zurich and as far afield as Stockholm until the late eighteenth century. In the 1750s the elongated, inventive and almost spiky designs of John Linnell did not appeal. But Linnell's coffee pot was eventually taken up by Robert Garrard in 1835 just when Rococo designs were being republished and the Louis XV revival was beginning. Thomas Stothard, designer for Rundell, Bridge & Rundell, drew on engravings by Jean le Pautre of the 1670s for candelabra, although they had to be modified considerably for manufacture in the first quarter of the nineteenth century.

Ideas migrated in many ways: sketches carried by journeymen, casting patterns in lead, brass or wood (rarely silver), printed engravings of ornament, the memory of an alert traveller with visual sensibility, or a novel object shown around. Actual objects could also be used as casting patterns. In the mid-eighteenth century New York and Jamaican silversmiths cast from London-made candlesticks. The same opportunistic spirit is responsible for an unusual set of casters with goat legs by Simon Pantin (1740) in the Victoria and Albert Museum. This exactly reproduces a set by Thomas Germain bought by an English nobleman some years earlier. Germain was proud of his model which was included, with a tureen and shell spice box, in a painting by Desportes. His tureen design was popular in London 30 years later, when Parker & Wakelin found its restrained lines fitted well the new Classical idiom.

The trade was quick to obtain visual references for a new look. When D'Hancarville's volumes of the Hamilton collection of ancient vases arrived in London, Louisa Courtauld obtained access to a copy and lifted both the shape and the Classical deities for sets of condiment vases in 1771. The diverse style we term 'Rococo' arrived in London in the early 1730s just when for the first time there were drawing academies that chasers and other artisans could attend. Asymmetrical cartouches, shellwork and fleshy contortions were creeping into plasterwork by the Atari family. Decorative painting by Gaetano Brunetti combined emblems of the seasons, the senses, the elements and naturalistic foliage and fruit familiar from 50 years earlier. Paul de Lamerie's unnamed, probably German-trained, designer mingled auricular forms, delicate figurework and cartouches while his contemporary Paul Crespin drew directly on recent French design and copied French silver from the Jewel House. De Lamerie clearly depended on earlier engravings, such as of vases by Fischer von Erlach or a frieze of 1618 reproduced in Augsburg about 1710, and he is not known to have travelled outside England. By contrast Thomas Germain, royal goldsmith to Louis XV, had been sent to study in Rome. His silver has a sculptural quality; it is monumental, well balanced and beautifully modelled.

To be 'in the new fashion' was a commonly expressed aspiration and a selling-point cited on trade cards, which were themselves a powerful means of advertising and fed a taste for such new motifs as cartouches. The written language of silver design was somewhat inexpressive: phrases such as 'curiously wrought', 'fair chased' or 'fine work' are not helpful as descriptions.

Engravers published designs that mixed current and older motifs. The box and flasks are a decade earlier
than the complex panel of mask and foliage.

Terms for distinct styles were rarely used until the nineteenth century, although the early sixteenth century brought in a new vocabulary: crotesk (grotesque), rabask (arabesque) and damask (damascene). The rich mix of images found on late Stuart silver, wallpaper and tapestries by John Vanderbank – figures in Persian costume, Classical ruins and fountains, pseudo-oriental trees and birds that we now call chinoiserie – was summed up as 'Japan' at the time. The order to De Lamerie and other goldsmiths commissioned to make new display plate for Goldsmiths' Hall in 1740 specified only 'proper ornaments'. When Neo-Classicism was becoming the prevailing style in the late 1760s, the silversmiths' ledgers refer only to a limited menu of gadroons, knurls and bagots. Much of the language of the artisan was expressed in visual rather than verbal terms.

At the top of polite society, silver was an essential element in rooms used for entertaining. Architects were expected to produce designs for the complete interior, from the candlesticks to the bed, from the centrepiece to the door furniture. It is no surprise to find, for example, Sir William Chambers publishing a design for a teapot or firedogs in the Chinese taste, or William Kent designing dish-covers or an inkstand for Queen Charlotte. These designs had then to be reworked to make them practicable for the silversmith, a task carried out in Chambers' drawing office by John Yenn. The silversmith might then further modify the design, to enable him to economize by using an existing casting pattern or because the structure was unstable. Matthew Boulton had for example to strengthen Wyatt's design for an epergne, after it had been made up.

However exciting it may be to study those objects that can be traced to their design roots, in most objects the design essence was simplified to enable it to be reproduced in batches by workmen with no aspiration to or training for invention. The bulk of goldsmiths' work is and always has been produced to a price, for sale to a known clientele wanting value for money. Extremes of design, whether cast or chased, cost the manufacturer more and were the exception. A Rococo scroll handle or Neo-Classical beading may have been the sole decorative element to catch the customer's eye but it could still capture the sense of current style.

For those who could not afford solid silver or gold, various imitations and substitutes have been produced since ancient times. An object made of base metal could be given the appearance of gold or silver given by plating the surface with a thin coating of these precious metals. Tin was also used as a plating material as it resembles silver when polished. Much brassware of the 17th and 18th centuries imitated the design of silver vessels, especially tablewares like cream jugs, basins and kettles. In the records of the Goldsmiths' Company there are numerous references to plated wares being passed off as sterling silver. London goldsmiths sold 'French plate', base metal coated with silver, for candelabra, dishcovers and toiletware. Sword-hilts could be deceptive as the hallmarks were difficult to find and the look and weight of base metal heavily plated with silver or mercury gilt

was very similar to solid silver.

During the 18th century some interesting alloys were used as substitutes for silver. One of these is 'paktong', which derives from the Chinese word *baitong*, an alloy of nickel, copper and zinc. This unusual alloy, which is shiny and varies in colour from yellow to silver, was first imported into England early in the 18th century. One of the most successful substitutes for

silver used in the later part of the 18th century was Sheffield plate, invented in 1742 by Thomas Boulsover (1705–88). He observed that copper and silver, when fused in unequal amounts, expanded together at a uniform rate under pressure. By using rollers it was possible to produce a laminated sheet of copper and silver to make into a variety of objects. The development of die-stamping in the 1740s was of particular advantage to the makers of Sheffield plate as the carefully cut steel dies could be used to stamp designs into the laminated sheets. The crisp raised motifs were particularly suited to Neo-Classical ornament in the Adam style. Some Sheffield-plate wares, such as the candlesticks of the 1790s, are just as attractive as their counterparts in sterling silver. A few makers, Matthew Boulton (1728–1809) was one, worked both in silver and Sheffield plate.

After 1840 the potential of electrotyping, the electrical deposition of metal in a mould, was quickly realized. Electrotype copies of silver- or gold-plated copper reproduce exactly the front surface of an original. The front of this copy of a 16th-century Spanish dish is perfect; the back is rough where the copper has built up.

This 1760s candlestick is made of the Chinese alloy 'paktong' or 'tutenag', which resembles silver in colour and weight. Recent research has established that many 'paktong' wares were made in China to European designs.

Some very elegant wares in the Neo-Classical style, like this sauce-boat, were produced in Sheffield plate in the 1780s.

In the 18th century some brasswares closely followed contemporary designs in silver. This brass English cream jug of about 1750 may have been passed off as silver as it has traces of silvering and is stamped with bogus hallmarks.

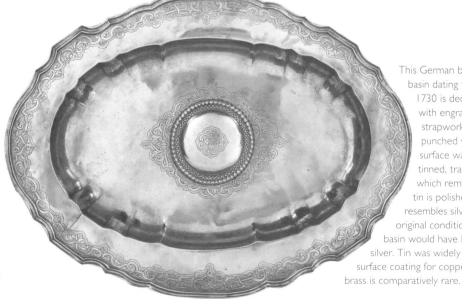

This German brass basin dating from about 1730 is decorated with engraved strapwork and punched work. The surface was originally tinned, traces of which remain. When tin is polished it resembles silver. In its original condition this basin would have looked like silver. Tin was widely used as a surface coating for copper; but on brass is comparatively rare.

SELLING SILVER

To sell high-value goods to a wealthy and fashion-conscious clientele, a goldsmith needed stylish, luxurious and secure premises. Shops began as extensions to traditional streetside displays of stock in front of the workshop but were radically transformed by the expansion of the retailing trade that took place during the seventeenth century. This resulted in more shops and new marketing strategies. Goldsmiths used trade cards to advertise themselves to a wider public, establish credentials and show what they could make. The design of the shop interior and window displays, and the use of large iron hanging signs or painted fascia boards, had a more immediate and local impact. The need for a specialized, and often costly, selling environment led increasingly to its separation from the production process. Most businesses selling gold and silver came to rely on a network of subcontractors and workshops at a distance to make most of their wares.

Elaborate shop fittings and a showy display of silver came to play a progressively more important role in securing sales. By 1650 Amsterdam goldsmiths' shops already demonstrated the sophistication necessary to attract and retain custom. Comfortable seating and attractive displays of silver and jewellery in purpose-built cases were as important as the general ambience created by the decoration. The thriving market for the decorative arts in Holland, where the competitive atmosphere was compounded by the growing discrimination of the shopper, may well have encouraged the Dutch to develop shops and shop design ahead of the rest of Europe. This lead was, however, to be challenged by the English and the French.

The inventories of English goldsmiths show that many were using a large number of expensive fittings in their shops from the beginning of the eighteenth century. Daniel Defoe's advice to the trade, *The Complete English Tradesman* (1726), describes the painting, carving and gilding, the use of fine shelves, shutters, glass, pediments and columns that could absorb two-thirds of a tradesman's capital before stock was bought. The trade card of the goldsmith Phillips Garden illustrates a sumptuous interior, one of the few surviving images of an eighteenth-century London shop. The Gothic screen and other details in the shop were an expensive attempt to echo the grander architectural schemes of public rooms and the private homes of the aristocracy. The shopkeeper hoped thus to put customers at their ease and indicate the fashionable nature of the establishment.

Large shop windows and impressive glass display cabinets filled with a rich array of silver tableware in the latest style helped to establish a goldsmith's credibility and reputation. The extensive use of glass was unique to the goldsmithing trade. Since the fourteenth century the Goldsmiths' Company had forbidden the sale of plate by artificial light to guard against fraud. Candles and lamps were not common until the late eighteenth century so good access to daylight in the form of wide windows and skylights was essential. While ceramics and cloth were displayed on open shelves, the glass casing both protected the silver and emphasized its high value and status. Drawers under display cabinets held jewellery, gold and small silver.

Defoe recommended that the 'modern custom' of extravagant fitting out of shops be tempered by common sense. He accepted that elaborate interiors

A customer choosing a salt in a Dutch goldsmith's shop, late 17th century.

Trade card of goldsmith Phillips Garden of London illustrating the interior of a mid-18th-century English shop.

were prevalent but advised that it was better to have a full shop than a fine shop. He believed that successful trade was founded upon good stock, chosen with discrimination and shown to best advantage by the shopkeeper. Once customers had been enticed into the shop by the various retailing devices of advertisements, trade cards and window displays or by the reputation of the goldsmith, it was important to retain their custom. A comfortable ambience, courteous and knowledgeable shop staff, some choice in product design and the reassurance of fashionable goods could ensure a customer's support over long periods of time. The Georgian goldsmith Joseph Brasbridge attested to the worth of retaining customers over many years in his memoirs *The Fruits of Experience* (1824). It was the loyalty of many of his clients that enabled him to trade successfully again after his bankruptcy. He had a clear idea of what constituted good business practice: 'Only get people to come to your shop, and when there, you can easily convince them that they cannot go to a better; do as well as the best, and better than most, and you will always be sure of customers.'

Who were these customers that goldsmiths courted so carefully? In the eighteenth century a high-class shop in the Haymarket or Lincoln's Inn Fields could expect to serve men and women from the professional and commercial classes as well as the gentry and aristocracy. The grandest customers might expect some exclusivity of service, which often involved the shopkeeper taking designs and samples to their homes, but many also found shopping a pleasurable pastime. Lady Caroline Fox wrote from Kensington to her sister Emily, Duchess of Leinster in Ireland, in 1764, 'Let me have any order you may have as I don't at all dislike jaunting to town.'

The challenge of serving such clients was addressed by the manufacturer Matthew Boulton in a letter to James Adam in 1770 in which he discusses the London market and the need for suitable exhibition spaces. He favoured an arrangement more on the Parisian model: 'a large elegant room upstairs without any other window than a skylight, by this sort of concealment you excite curiosity more...The Nobility like that less public repository, the novelty would please more and last longer.' Some goldsmiths provided a separate entrance for their most important customers. Balancing provision for the needs of this group with the desire for greater overall custom was a dilemma for all shopkeepers. The potter Josiah Wedgwood reserved some viewing days at the beginning of his exhibitions for the nobility. Writing to his agent in London in 1794, Boulton emphasized the importance of the mass market: 'We think it of far more consequence to supply the people than the nobility only; and though you speak contemptuously of Hawkers, Pedlars and those who supply Petty Shops, yet we must own that we think they will do more towards supporting a great Manufactory, than all the Lords in the Nation.'

The possession of silver and imitation silver products moved further down the social scale so that by the end of the eighteenth century the poorest female labourer might own a spoon. Technical innovations had decreased the weight and therefore the cost of some silverware and new products such as Sheffield plate were up to a fifth cheaper than solid silver objects. The middle or poorer sections of society acquired their silver either in the capital at downmarket shops which offered a choice of finished goods of a standard type at the lowest fixed prices, or at provincial goldsmith's which sold good-quality local wares or bought silver from London and (as Lowe's of Chester or Langlands of Newcastle did) marked it as their own.

By the nineteenth century the shop had become the key form of retailing. Large multi-storeyed premises sold a range of standardized silver products from silver to electroplate. Customer choice, from a selection of ready-made comparable products, had replaced the earlier mode of shopping in which reliance on the advice of the shopkeeper was paramount.

Silver was also bought from trade outlets less specialized than goldsmiths' shops. Circulating libraries, particularly in the fashionable spa towns, increased their income through the sale of silver vessels, jewellery and trinkets. Small silver and Sheffield plate goods such as buckles, spoons and snuffboxes were sold through the agency of itinerant salesmen, fairs and markets. Men and women would sometimes band together in clubs for the express purpose of purchasing silver, mainly in the

Mappin Brothers' new shop in Regent Street, London, 1862.

form of small personal items such as spoons or watches. Silver could also be acquired by winning rather than purchasing. In Flanders, lotteries with silver plate as prizes date from as early as 1490 and silver was included in the earliest known English state lottery of 1567. Silver could be won as race or sporting prizes, presented as a token of thanks or esteem or inherited on the death of a relative.

Hall's circulating library showing silver and plated goods for sale, Margate, 1789.

In 1735 George Wickes moved to Panton Street off the Haymarket and opened a goldsmithing business called the King's Arms and Feathers, which became one of the largest and most prosperous in London. From its foundation it developed through a succession of partnerships: from 1750 George Wickes and Samuel Netherton; from 1760 John Parker (Samuel Netherton's second cousin, apprenticed to Wickes in 1751) and Edward Wakelin; from 1776 John Wakelin (Edward's son) and William Paris Tayler; and on Tayler's death in 1792 John Wakelin and Robert Garrard. Many successful goldsmithing businesses relied on similar dynastic structures, for example the Courtaulds and the Batemans in the second half of the 18th century. Although Robert Campbell in his *London Tradesman* (1747) warned of the problems of partnerships, they were a practical means of dividing the costs of setting up and running a business. Campbell, and Collyer in his *Parents and Guardians Directory* (1761), estimated that

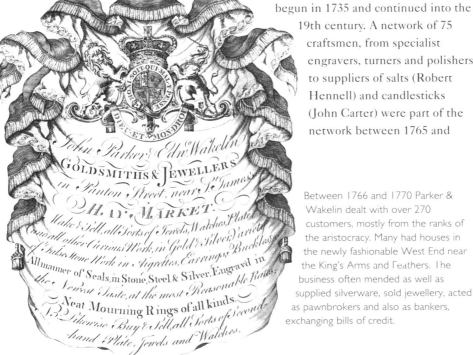

between £500 and £3,000 was required to start in the goldsmiths' trade. The raw material was expensive (silver was 5s. 6d an ounce in the 18th century), customers expected long periods of credit and bankruptcy was rife.

The story of the Panton Street firm is preserved in an unrivalled set of business accounts dealing with clients (Gentlemen's Ledgers) and manufacturers (Workmen's Ledgers), begun in 1735 and continued into the 19th century. A network of 75 craftsmen, from specialist engravers, turners and polishers to suppliers of salts (Robert Hennell) and candlesticks (John Carter) were part of the network between 1765 and

Dru Drury, like other retail goldsmiths in 18th-century London, depended on a closely related collectivity of workshops tied together by reliance on each other's skills. This was in large part what the notion of a trade meant in the 18th century.

1770. The 'maker's mark' on a piece of silver could refer to any of the specialists involved in its production or the retailer, depending on who was responsible for taking the silver to the Assay Office. The tea tub opposite illustrates how subcontractors worked. John Ansill and Stephen Gilbert made the body using 'small-working' techniques of scoring, folding and soldering ready-flattened silver sheet, a quick and easy method of manufacture compared with hand-raising.

Between 1766 and 1770 Parker & Wakelin dealt with over 270 customers, mostly from the ranks of the aristocracy. Many had houses in the newly fashionable West End near the King's Arms and Feathers. The business often mended as well as supplied silverware, sold jewellery, acted as pawnbrokers and also as bankers, exchanging bills of credit.

The firm bought in goods made by silversmiths in Sheffield (Tudor & Leader and John Winter) and Birmingham (Boulton & Fothergill). The Panton Street shop was the retailing centre and the partners often struck their own mark over that of the supplier.

Many subcontractors would be involved in fulfilling a client's order. The dinner service made for Lord Harcourt between 1768 and 1769 brought in specialist makers of knives and forks, suppliers of plates and dishes, and those like Thomas Pitts who made mainly tureens and epergnes. The subcontracting network operated not only for such large composite orders but also for individual objects.

What emerges from the Parker & Wakelin ledgers is a highly efficient network of subcontractors co-ordinated by the partners of the firm acting as retailers rather than manufacturers. It stretched from the locality of the shop in the West End, to the environs of Foster Lane around Goldsmiths' Hall.

Aaron and William Lestourgeon fitted a lock and lined Ansill & Gilbert's tea tub with lead. Robert Clee engraved the Chinese figures and a border. The silk-lined wooden case was supplied by Edward Smith. The cost to the client included payment to all these specialists, as well as the retailer's profit.

ATTITUDES TO SILVER

Ewer (above) and basin (opposite) with the arms of Queen Anne, lent to Lord Raby in 1705 for his Prussian embassy.

GIFTS, PRIZES AND REWARDS

My lord took a bowl of gold (which was esteemed at the value of 500 marks) and filled with hypocrass (whereof there was plenty) putting off his Cap said 'I drinketh to the King [Henry VIII] and to the King your master' [Francis I] and therewith drank a good draft. He then gave him the cup.

WOLSEY'S ENTERTAINMENT OF THE FRENCH AMBASSADORS, 1527

The exchange of gifts of silver is a phenomenon strictly regulated by long-standing tradition (see 'The Middle Ages'). At New Year, to mark rites of passage, to commemorate or reward, as entry fine or perquisite, the giving away of gold and silver plate has always been honourable, worthy of comment and an essential ingredient of society and obligation. It has also been good business for goldsmiths. Many gifts of plate were preserved from the melting pot and treasured for their associations. To increase the compliment to the recipient, the form of gift plate was often unusually lavish, elaborate and fashionable, like the magnificent gilt ewer and basin, richly chased with the latest Rococo motifs, which the City of Bristol presented to its Recorder John Scrope in 1736 (Al-Tajir Collection). Public gifts of plate have always received attention from diarists and journalists.

The spiral of gift-giving began at the top of society as, by convention, the monarch was expected to be open-handed. Almost every diplomatic contact was marked by an exchange of plate in public, although from the late seventeenth century a diamond-studded jewel became the preferred royal gift to an envoy. When James I needed to conclude a peace treaty with Spain in 1604, he raided the Jewel House to make a princely gesture to the various noble commissioners: the Count of Arenburg, who represented Archduke Albert of the Spanish Netherlands, received 1,000 ounces, all of which came from Henry VIII's Jewel House. What was presented was not necessarily new. The medieval Royal Gold Cup (now in the British Museum) was later presented by its recipient, the Constable of Castile, to a Spanish convent. This history of treasures passing from one collection to another reinforces the status of gift-plate as a symbol of munificence. Most of the large display pieces presented or sold to the tsars of Russia between the 1550s and the 1670s to sweeten trading relationships were decidedly second-hand. The well-known leopard pots had been made in 1600 and were striking, flashy and suited the known taste of the Russian monarchs; they had accumulated a menagerie of silvergilt animals and birds from their Danish, Hamburg and English envoys.

Reciprocity was an important feature of this practice. At New Year the monarch expected from all royal servants a present of goldsmiths' work carefully considered to reflect the interests of the recipient and the standing of the donor. Lord Lisle's London agent wrote a vivid description of Henry VIII leaning on a cupboard assessing everything as it was presented and listed in

Probably the earliest gold race prize, this 1675 cup descended in the Bowes-Lyon family.

full view of the court: 'The King's Maiestie receaved right joyously.' In return each donor received a set weight of plate from the Jewel House (30 to 33 ounces for an earl, far less costly than that handed over as a gift). These royal gifts, like the Sterne Cup (1673), were often treasured and mentioned in wills. Charles II abolished the custom of New Year gifts in 1680.

From the sixteenth century ambassadors, as the representatives of the Crown, established a claim to be equipped with several thousand ounces of plate. But the crown found it hard to recall these loans as the great Whig families strengthened their grip on the wheels of government. Until the system was abolished as part of the Duke of Wellington's reforms in the 1820s, royal officials or their heirs could obtain a writ under Privy Seal converting the loan to a gift. Although this could cost £150 in fees, among those who considered it a small outlay to acquire title were the Earl of Chesterfield, who acquired a service of plate including wine coolers by Paul Crespin, and the Duke of Bedford, when he obtained a dinner service in 1771.

Reviving a Roman tradition vividly expressed in Mantegna's *Triumphs of Caesar*, military leaders were often rewarded with magnificent services, which were publicly displayed. When the Portuguese Service

arrived in London in 1817, Garrard's, goldsmiths to the Duke of Wellington, arranged an exhibition at their Panton Street premises. 'Persons of honour' entering a city would be greeted with lavish entertainment, processions, music and a gift of plate, often a cup filled with gold coins 'to manifest the city's love!' When Charles I travelled north for his ill-fated Scottish coronation in 1633, he accumulated civic gifts on route: Leicester, for example gave him a gilt ewer and basin. Generosity was expected in return. The Earl of Yarmouth, visiting Great Yarmouth in 1675, was greeted with gunfire, bellringing and speeches. At the dinner, the Earl 'set a bottle at every man's trencher...we parted with that they call starke love and kindness.'

Prizes for sporting achievement have a long history that originates with the gold and silver wreaths of the ancient world. In the Middle Ages skill with a bow and arrow, and later with a gun, was necessary for national defence. Shooting competitions were a regular feature of civic life and winners' names were often recorded on a corporately owned piece of plate. But the sport that attracted the richest flow of precious metal into private hands was horse racing. The silver spurs and bells offered as prizes in the sixteenth century (a rare survival are two silver bells belonging to Carlisle) gave way from the Restoration to two-handled cups with covers. The two-handled cup, a newly fashionable form of plate peculiar to England, was ideal for convivial drinking and perhaps mistily recalled Classical tradition. Prize cups were displayed near the winning post and passed round so the owners could share the spiced wine, cider or punch. This enjoyable practice rapidly dictated the most popular form of plate for prizes, although monteiths and punch bowls were also offered. Ladies' races had different prizes: tankards, coffeepots or teapots. In 1707 Thomas Cave boasted about a win at Lutterworth races: 'My Deare had entered my horse, by virtue of his fleet heales he wone the Tankard, which is a very good one to drink Asses' Milk out of, it being somewhat large.' (Asses' milk was recommended for women and invalids.) Two-handled cups or urns became the standard for most types of prize, such as the famous Patriotic Fund vases, pecuniary or honourable rewards or badges of distinction given for distinguished service during the Napoleonic War. Seventy-three vases and 10 other pieces of plate were awarded between 1803 when the fund was established and 1809.

The English retained a passion for presentation silver and an astonishing variety and range of large prizes and testimonial pieces emerged in the nineteenth century. But, as Charles Eastlake and others regretfully observed, many of them were in effect merely 'vehicles for the employment of so many ounces of bullion'.

Livery companies, colleges, ships, regiments, clubs of all sorts and indeed virtually all masculine societies, accumulated plate for their corporate life, much of it for drinking. Custom dictated that fellow-commoners at the Oxford and Cambridge colleges, and the sons of Roman Catholics studying at St Omer or Douai, presented a beaker, goblet or mug, which formed a reservoir of plate for corporate use in emergencies. When Queen's College in Cambridge had to select plate to sacrifice for the King in 1642, all but three of the 72 pieces were accumulated drinking vessels and none of the founders' plate was touched. Members of livery companies paid fines of plate if they failed to fulfil their obligations. The York Silk Weavers' Company when regulating its annual feast in 1665

This cup, a prize at Doncaster races in 1857, stands more than two feet (60cm) tall.

required a piece of plate worth at least 30 shillings (enough to buy three or four spoons or a cup) from the Warden if he failed to provide a gallon of claret. When Sir Robert Vyner was Sheriff of London the Goldsmiths' Company lent him plate for his official entertainments. In return he gave a silver bell (1666), now in an inkstand made by Paul de Lamerie in 1741. These corporate collections, which were created by individual generosity and have largely been kept together in England, are relatively little known as a source of antique plate. Similar traditions prevailed throughout Europe but no other country has preserved so much of its civic and institutional silver.

Left: The present Goldsmiths' Hall in Foster Lane, off Cheapside, was designed by Philip Hardwick and opened in 1835. It is externally much the same today and sees active use by the Company and other organizations.

Below left: The Bowes Cup (1554), used by Queen Elizabeth I at her coronation banquet in 1558, was given to Sir Martin Bowes as the perquisite of the Lord Mayor of London. This silvergilt standing cup and cover is the oldest piece with a continuous history in the Company's ownership. It survives because of its special association as a gift from Sir Martin Bowes, Prime Warden of the Company in 1581.

Below: The Amity Cup (1982), which honours the ancient friendship between the Companies of Fishmongers and Goldsmiths, was designed and made by Kevin Coates, one of Britain's foremost goldsmiths. It was commissioned by Professor R.Y. Goodden, former Pro-Rector of the Royal College of Art, to commemorate his year as Prime Warden of the Company, 1976–77.

Opposite left: This virtuoso work by Jane Short, an enamelled vase inspired by a jay's wing, was commissioned for the Company's collection. It led to her being asked to produce work for Lichfield Cathedral. Another piece by Short is in the V&A.

Opposite top right: Water jug by Shannon O'Neill, graduate winner of the Worshipful Company of Goldsmiths' Young Designer–Silversmith Competition in 1995. This award encourages studio silver design in a London workshop and is open to any student under 30 on an approved course.

Opposite bottom right: Necklace in 18 carat gold, black enamel and Wedgwood black basalt (1984) by Wendy Ramshaw OBE. It was commissioned from this studio jeweller for the Company's collection of innovative modern jewellery following her 1982 exhibition at the V&A held in collaboration with Wedgwood.

The special character of the Worshipful Company of Goldsmiths is a result of its long history (over 650 years) and its engagement with the present. The Company received its first royal charter in 1327 and is a living successor of the guild system found throughout Europe in the Middle Ages. Besides continuing its centuries-old statutory function of hallmarking, the Company promotes high standards for those craftsmen working in silver, gold and platinum. Since the 1950s three generations of art jewellers and art medallists have often received their first commission from the Company. Goldsmiths' Hall in the heart of the City of London houses an outstanding collection of 8,000 pieces from the 15th century to the present. most of which bear London hallmarks. All categories of the collection – antique and domestic silver, contemporary silver, jewellery and medals – have either been used for their original purpose or were commissioned for display to inspire patronage. This policy of enhancing the standing of the Company through the display of fine silver was initiated by ordinance in 1469. In the course of the following 200 years the collection was primarily used as a reserve fund in times of need, for example the Civil War and the Great Fire. Only silver that had special associations with the Company survived. The recommendation in 1736 that 3,406 ounces of plate, a small part of what had been sold or melted down in the previous century, should be replaced gave the Company a number of excellent Rococo pieces all made between 1740 and 1741, including the magnificent silvergilt basin and ewer by Paul de Lamerie.

The Company bought dining silver from the royal goldsmiths Rundell, Bridge & Rundell for the opening of the new Goldsmiths' Hall in 1835. Historic silver has continued to be acquired in the 20th century although in recent years the Company has directed its funds towards supporting living craftsmen. The modern collections are recognized as outstanding examples of creative vitality, setting high standards as catalysts for our future heritage.

COLLECTING

These antique, well-preserved pieces, so Mr Jeffries said, often find a purchaser more readily than the modern. This is because the English are fond of constructing and decorating whole portions of their country houses, or at least one large apartment, in old Gothic style, and are glad to purchase any accessories dating from the same or a similar period.

DESCRIPTION BY SOPHIE VON LA ROCHE, A GERMAN VISITOR TO LONDON, OF THE SECOND-HAND PLATE IN THE SHOWROOMS OF THE ROYAL GOLDSMITH THOMAS JEFFERYS, 1786

The concept of the collector as we understand it today did not properly emerge until the eighteenth century. Before this silver was collected for its economic, social or religious associations rather than for the aesthetic motives that fire the connoisseur. Silver has always been prized for the status and financial security it confers, which is why it was so readily re-made to keep abreast of fashion, or melted down in times of need. Silver collections were often accumulated through a passive process of gift, inheritance and as a result of social obligation.

None the less collections of silver were assembled. The Church had changing needs for liturgical plate, and traditionally the financial status of ecclesiastical institutions was often partly vested in their treasuries. The Emperor Constantine established a pattern (still in existence today) of lay gifts of silver to the Church after his conversion to Christianity in 312 AD. Developments in the early liturgy also prompted the accumulation of silver. The sanctioning of the display of relics in 867 led to the invention of richly worked reliquaries, often the most costly items in the treasury, to be exhibited on the altar. There are some exceptions to the piecemeal accumulation of objects. The Treasury of the Abbey of St Denis in Paris was systematically equipped by Abbot Suger during the 1140s and his accounts show that he deliberately selected the most prestigious pieces available, such as the vessel of rock-crystal, a royal wedding gift to Louis VII in 1137, which Suger had mounted in gold.

In the secular world there are several examples of enlightened patrons who seem to have collected as much out of an interest in the objects themselves as for social reasons. Jean, Duc de Berri stands out, as do his brothers Charles V of France and Louis, Duc d'Orléans whose inventory ran to some 4,000 pieces of goldsmiths' work, most presumably intended for the buffet. Otherwise, those who could afford it bought, gave and received silver in response to domestic needs and social obligations. Livery companies and colleges acquired plate through members' gifts and fines, although their collections were not immune from refashioning or sale if necessary. Why one object was kept when another was given away or sent to the melt was a matter of personal preference, but mounted objects had a curiosity value and often survived when larger domestic plate did not.

In the mid-sixteenth century, there was a marked shift towards the acquisition of costly or curious objects which were displayed together to demonstrate the taste and learning of the owner. A cabinet of curiosities (*Kunstkammer*, *Schatzkammer* or *Wunderkammer*) containing rare and precious objects, but also natural curiosities, rapidly became an essential status symbol for major patrons (see 'Mannerism'). In 1565 Duke Albrecht of Bavaria acknowledged the significance of

Conversazione and exhibition of works of art at Ironmongers' Hall in 1861, *Illustrated London News.*

his collection by designating 45 objects in his treasury 'inalienable heirlooms', the foundation of a collection that remains to this day in the Residenzmuseum in Munich. He was followed by the Elector Augustus I of Saxony and Emperor Rudolph II who established their *Kunstkammern* in 1560 and the 1580s in Dresden and Prague respectively. This phenomenon was not confined to the continent of Europe. The contents of the Jewel House at the Tower of London were displayed to distinguished foreign visitors in the late sixteenth century and English collectors such as Sir Walter Cope and the earls of Yarmouth assembled exotic collections. In the seventeenth century Thomas Howard, Earl of Arundel (d. 1646), one of the first English collectors in the modern sense, whose collection included 'silvergilt plate, crystal vases, agat cups' was still the exception rather than the rule. However,

the importance of some historic plate was recognized. In 1644 the House of Lords blocked a motion to melt the Tudor plate from the Jewel House because of its associations and craftsmanship. These old display pieces were subsequently snapped up by European collectors. Similar sentiments were applied to college plate, particularly if objects were thought (albeit sometimes wrongly) to have a connection with founders.

Interest in historic plate developed slowly through the eighteenth century. The mounted porcelain vase of 1665 by Wolfgang Hauser was retained at Stowe by the Temple family and displayed first in the State Bedchamber and then in the Duchess's Drawing Room until the sale in 1848. In 1791 the Musée des Monuments Français opened to the public. Established by Alexandre Lenoir, it displayed a range of medieval and Renaissance antiquities most of which had been dispersed from Church ownership during the Revolution. It was itself broken up after the defeat of Napoleon. At the same time a market for antique silver began to develop to meet the needs of the new connoisseurs. The *Gentleman's Magazine* published articles on old silver from the 1760s. Frequent references to old plate in the advertisements and trade cards of pawnbrokers and goldsmiths tell the same story. The taste for historic objects was fostered by learned societies (the Society of Antiquaries was founded in 1707 and formally established in 1717) and collectors who created antiquarian interiors, such as Horace Walpole (1717–97) at Strawberry Hill and William Beckford at Fonthill Abbey in Wiltshire. Beckford's commissions to contemporary silversmiths for historicizing pieces were

This jar was probably exhibited off the State Bedroom at Stowe from the 1730s, along with other mounted exotica.

part of a general attempt by goldsmiths and their customers to exploit old styles during the Regency.

The enthusiasm for collecting applied art, including silver, was largely the creation of the nineteenth century. Apart from the antique plate sold by goldsmiths such as Rundell's, the dispersal on to the market of important collections (Duke of Norfolk, 1816; Beckford's Fonthill, 1823; Duke of York, 1827; Walpole's Strawberry Hill, 1842) stimulated the increasing demand for the fashionable late seventeenth-century English and continental buffet and furnishing plate. German silvergilt of the sixteenth and seventeenth centuries was particularly sought after. It became financially worthwhile for goldsmiths to 'improve' old plate by adding extra and often very showy chasing. The cataloguing of sales was rudimentary. Collectors and dealers often had very little hard evidence for attribution. This situation gradually improved under the influence of exhibitions, museums, new publications and societies devoted to the systematic study of historic art objects.

The exhibition *Works of Ancient and Medieval Art*, held by the Society of Arts in 1850, was the first opportunity for the English public to see a large gathering of antique silver. In 1851 the antiquarian Octavius Morgan MP publicized the full meaning of marks on English silver. He knew that they could reveal the date and place of manufacture as well as act as the guarantees of silver content, which his fellow-collectors had thought was their only function. Morgan's work inspired many others including the dealer William Chaffers, who published *Hall Marks on Gold and Silver Plate* in 1863 and Wilfred Cripps, whose *Old English Plate* (1878) had reached its eighth edition at his death in 1903.

Probably the first exhibition where silver hallmarks were explained was the *Conversazione* at Ironmongers' Hall in 1861. Chaffers was on the committee and lenders included 24 livery companies, dealers and private individuals such as John Dunn-Gardner, whose

Elaborately mounted shells were much prized by collectors from the 16th century onwards, and the nautilus shell was particularly popular.

collection was on loan to the Victoria and Albert Museum from 1870 to 1901. Opportunities for collectors to see antique plate had increased enormously since 1850. The foundation of the Museum of Ornamental Art (later the Victoria and Albert Museum) in 1852 at Marlborough House, the establishment of medieval and later collections at the British Museum by the curator A.W. Franks and the continuing success of exhibitions of historic objects such as those in Manchester in 1857 and in London in 1862 confirmed the scale of interest in the applied arts.

For some years from 1857 the Fine Arts Club, the brainchild of J.C. Robinson, first curator of art at the embryonic Victoria and Albert Museum, supplied this need. As museum collections began to grow, there were greater opportunities for collectors to inform their approach to the subject. Bodies such as the Antique Plate Committee and the Society of Silver Collectors (now the Silver Society) were established in the 1930s and 1958 resepctively. The increasingly fruitful relationship between museums, private individuals and the trade has resulted in a constant re-evaluation of objects and their history. Arthur Grimwade's *London Goldsmiths 1697–1837* and Sir Charles Jackson's *English Goldsmiths and Their Lives* are two examples of the enormous benefits of this collaboration.

Gold and silver wares, because of their intrinsic value, have been copied to deceive for centuries. Base metals such as copper, bronze and brass were gilded or silvered and struck with pseudo-hallmarks in order to be passed off as genuine works. Once old silver was collectable it rapidly became one of the most attractive areas for fakers. Plain wares have been redecorated to increase their market appeal and the form of a vessel changed into something rarer and more expensive, such as the Elizabethan chalice which turned into an early coffee pot. Steel punches were specially cut to forge rare early hallmarks or the marks of well-known makers. When engraving, especially heraldry, becomes worn it can be re-cut. Extensive repairs can be disguised with gilding or silver plating. Electrotype copies of gold and silver have been successfully passed off as the real thing. Genuine but plain wares can be given a false provenance to enhance their market value, or an engraved coat of arms from an interesting family to aid the deception. Pieces can be created copying old designs by artists such as Hans Holbein.

It is not only very ornate display wares that are faked; false copies of more humble articles such as cutlery and corkscrews are also made. Wealthy collectors often lay themselves open to

Spoons have been popular collector's items since the late 18th century. Seen together, it is evident that these English spoons in late 17th-century style must be recent casts from a genuine example as all the hallmarks are identically located.

forgers when they try to collect in a field where there is little to choose from. A surprising feature of recent fakes in precious metal is the number and variety of wares made in gold. These include not only enamelled snuff-boxes but also entire services. Some of the most successful forgeries have been aimed at specific collectors whose tastes are known. In recent years the standard of craftsmanship of forgeries in gold and silver has been so high that metallurgical analysis is often the only way to distinguish the genuine piece.

This silvergilt figure of the Virgin and Child, supposedly French of about 1400, was one of the great treasures of the V&A. However recent metallurgical analysis has established beyond doubt that it was made in the 19th century. The forger has used a 14th-century French ivory statuette as the model.

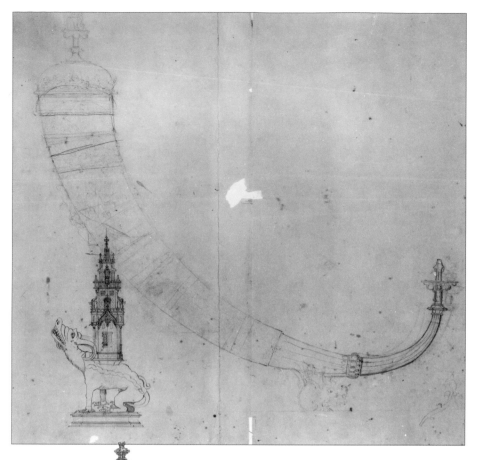

These designs for a large drinking-horn in the 15th-century style are by the Aachen goldsmith and forger Reinhold Vasters (1827–1909), who specialized in jewellery and enamelled wares in the Renaissance style. The discovery of a large number of designs by Vasters in the V&A has led to the attribution of many so-called 16th-century wares to his workshop. Such finds are exceptionally rare as forgers are naturally secretive about their activities.

This fine-looking stoneware jug is fitted with embossed and chased silvergilt mounts. The mounts are struck with London hallmarks for 1576–77 and the maker's mark WC above a grasshopper. When the stoneware jug was tested by thermoluminescence, it was revealed that it actually dated from about 1800.

A plain 18th-century bowl was converted to a late 17th-century two-handled cup in about 1890. The body has been engraved, embossed with swirling flutes and two cast handles attached. The work is far too coarse to be genuine and the proportions of the vessel are incorrect.

Marks are frequently faked or altered. A piece of silver bearing London hallmarks for 1569–70 has been cut out of a genuine Elizabethan object and reshaped to fit round the neck of a fake stoneware jug. The other two marks have been added in order to lend authenticity to the confection.

Silver has a good second-hand market It has always been bought in prosperity and sold in times of hardship. *By Order of the Court* portrays the mixed emotions attached to the phrase 'selling the family silver'. The excitement of the bidders and the lively movement of the auctioneer is juxtaposed with the melancholy air of the couple to the left of the painting, perhaps the owners of the shining silver on the auctioneer's table.

This line drawing of London hallmarks appeared in the first issue of *The Connoisseur*. The author of the article 'Hallmarks on Old English Silver' warned collectors of the alterations and improvements made to silver through generations of ownership, citing a Jacobean tankard with 19th-century chasing as a bad investment.

This French vinaigrette is gold and silvergilt. George IV's daughter, Princess Charlotte, threw it into the fire in temper. It was rescued by the doner's ancestor who worked in the royal household.

'In the narrow streets of cities, up and down thro mart and store/On the outlook still for treasures lost upon Times shifting shore.' The opening verse in the first issue of *The Connoisseur* (1901) evokes a romantic vision of the collector combing darkened Dickensian streets looking for the hidden, undervalued or undiscovered. Collecting has a long history in England and the *Gentleman's Magazine* published collectors' queries about apostle spoons, for example, as early as the 1760s. Times have changed and people are now generally more aware of the value of things but treasures can still be found. Often not fully hallmarked, small silverwork can be bought relatively cheaply at bric-a-brac stalls, charity shops, antique markets and fairs as well as at auction and in antique shops.

Small silverwork has always been of particular interest to the collector because of its infinite inventiveness of form, decoration and usage. Thimbles, bottle tickets, caddy spoons and snuffboxes all illustrate work of equal skill to that expended on larger and more expensive objects. Groups such as the Silver Society and Wine Label Circle (see 'Societies and Periodicals') publish research in their own periodicals and meet to discuss questions prompted by their own collections and silver issues of wider concern.

Thanks to the gifts and bequests of collectors, the V&A has unrivalled collections of smallwork, which provide a basis of study for both the specialist and those beginning a collection. Cropper's collection of bottle tickets and wine labels, the Fitzhenry Collection of caddy spoons, fish trowels and snuffers, and the nutmeg graters amassed by Guy and Rupert Oswald-Smith are only three of a number of collections that have enriched the Museum. These collections cannot be displayed in their entirety but are available for study by appointment.

Despite their small size, the decoration and design of bottle tickets and wine labels accurately reflect changing styles and tastes in drinks from the early 18th century. Long-forgotten concoctions such as Hungary Water, 'a spiritous medicament seldom or never us'd inwardly' (1725) can lead to interesting research.

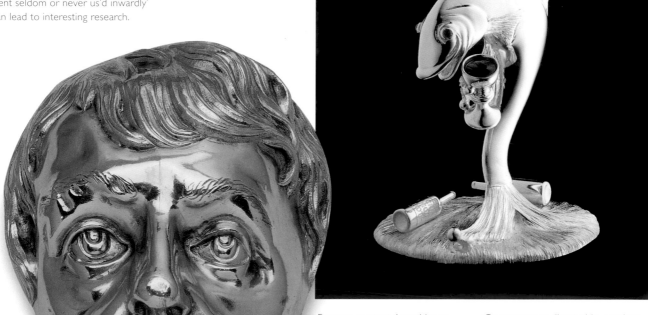

From monumental trophies to simple spoons, commemorative items in silver incorporate motifs particular to the historic event or person. This tobacco box commemorates the victories and death of Admiral Lord Nelson. It is cast as his death mask and set with a piece of oak from his ship, HMS *Bellerophon*.

Contemporary silversmiths continue to find a market for small collectable silver. Boxes, spoons, flasks and toilet wares are all functional but can be witty too, as is this goblet from the Sarah Jones Studio entitled *Drinking Like a Fish*.

CEREMONY AND AUTHORITY

Eyes are fixed on relics covered with gold, and purses are opened. The thoroughly beautiful image of some saint is believed to be the more holy the more highly coloured the image is. People rush to kiss it, they are invited to donate, and they admire the beautiful more than they venerate the sacred... What do you think is being sought in all this?

ST BERNARD OF CLAIRVAUX,
APOLOGIA AD GUILLIELMUM ABBATEM, 1125

The rare and costly metals of silver and gold have been the first choice for ceremonial objects and symbols of authority since early times. Lustrous, heavy, solid yet malleable, able to reflect candle flame or sunlight from its burnished surface, silver in particular has been worked up into maces and staves, reliquaries and candle-holders or vessels for purification and communal rites in almost all societies and religious groups. Much of the energy in contemporary silver studies is concerned with social or design history and consequently these symbols of authority or of worship have been marginalized. In a secular world, where tradition is losing its value, they speak more quietly. Although some are rarely seen and little appreciated beyond a shrinking circle, they retain symbolic power.

When in 1976 Michael Heseltine flourished the Speaker's Mace in the House of Commons in a dramatic gesture, he was handling a powerful symbol of authority whose origins lay in an Anglo-Saxon offensive weapon.

One of the 20 or so mace-bearers in the coronation procession of James II, 1685.

London's Lord Mayor's Show, the annual display of civic pageantry that now gives pleasure to tourists, originally had the serious purpose of proclaiming and asserting hard-won privileges. When the mayor appears in public he is accompanied by his mace-bearer, who carries on his shoulder a Great Mace of silver with an arched crown at end and at the other a faceted knob. The latter is the last vestige of the original lethal weapon of iron carried by the Crown's sergeant-at-arms. Edward III granted the City of London the privilege of a mace-bearing escort of sergeants-at-arms empowered to arrest wrong-doers. By the late seventeenth century this symbol of royal power had been widely adopted as corporations, wards and other organizations asserted their self-confidence and delegated authority. Maces were re-made, enlarged and duplicated, valued not only as a symbol of authority but also as an index of standing. The considerable cost in metal and workmanship was ungrudgingly met, sometimes as a gift from a nobleman concerned with local politics and sometimes by subscription. A mace of 1663 in the Victoria and Albert Museum was given by the Duke of Bedford to the Bedford Level Conservators, a group of investors (of whom he was one) who were to administer the newly drained district. As civic reforms in the early nineteenth century swept away old administrative systems, so their silver became redundant. The

Silver, gilding, enamel and jewels beautified the magnificent Three Kings Shrine in Cologne Cathedral, which would have been glimpsed by candlelight.

Harcourt collection at the Museum of London contains several hundred maces and staves of office of English, European and more distant origins. The last vestige of the Court Leet of St Andrew Holborn, its mace, was given to the Victoria and Albert Museum in 1897, 'the proceedings for which it met having either become unnecessary or taken over by some other tribunal.' It had been made by Benjamin Pyne in 1694 from cups, a salt and an older mace given over the years since 1612.

Because they have left a rich documentary trail, maces and other civic silver can show how goldsmiths operated. At Wilton near Salisbury in 1639 a new mace was ordered from the local goldsmith Richard Grafton, who had his name engraved on it. But the mace was actually made and marked by John Greene, another Salisbury goldsmith. When new maces were ordered a

century later, the local goldsmith sent the order to the Londoner Gabriel Sleath. The maces were heavy (more than 300 ounces) and costly at 11s. 6d an ounce plus 2s. 6d more per ounce for gilding, but their central role in civic life made this a light burden. Staves of office and verger's wands with silver heads were in common use as symbols of authority on public occasions from the sixteenth century; the glint of light on the metal helped them to be visible at a distance in a crowd. Those with some official standing such as king's messengers, almsmen and Thames watermen and porters were issued with silver badges.

There have always been two aspects to the use of silver in worship. Underlying its proclaimed purpose in protecting the sacred elements or the holy word, containing offerings, concentrating the worshipper's attention, assisting ritual absolutions and so on, has been the significance of silver in alluding to and symbolizing the beauty of holiness and the purity of the divine. Although from time to time liturgical silver has been seized, melted down, sold or turned to profane purposes, there has been in all societies a stubborn restatement of these metaphorical associations. When ritual objects are reluctantly sold because a church or synagogue has come to the end of its resources, a value beyond the financial and antique continues to accrue to them. The newly opened Jewish Museum in London displays beautiful examples of ritual silver made in the past 300 years and treasuries in cathedrals across England display Anglican and in a few places Nonconformist and Roman Catholic silver. And silver for worship is still commissioned. However, some believers feel uneasy about this careful attention to historic treasures, which is seen as diverting resources that could be used to alleviate poverty. The medieval illustration of the Virgin, giving the gifts of the Magi to the poor, expresses this ancient and continuing choice.

A recurrent dilemma for the Christian Church in its attitude towards art and ritual has been whether to imitate the renunciate nature of Christ or glorify him as King and Saviour. Although renunciation and glorification are not mutually exclusive, they become so when silver is the means of expression. For several centuries after Christ, the objects used in the Eucharist were simply a means to an end. The material and form were not specified so household utensils were used, as for the Jewish Passover, which is celebrated in a domestic setting, and the Last Supper, which took place at a Passover feast. Wood and glass were as common as precious and other metals. The use of precious metal for ritual objects other than the essential chalice and paten came later in the Middle Ages with the development of censers to purify the ritual space during services, incense boats to store incense, ewers to hold water for the ritual washing of the celebrant's hands, pyxes and ciboria to contain the unused Host, and many other utensils.

A ritual object was not only a recipient of veneration but also a means of expressing veneration. The making

or donation of church embellishments was highly respected. Abbot Suger eloquently described his abundant patronage of the Abbey of St Denis as an expression of his praise. An inscription on the cover of a gospel book in the Treasury of the Convent of Notre-Dame in Namur describes how for its maker, the goldsmith Hugo of Oignies, the act of creation was itself a form of prayer: 'Others praise Christ with their voices; Hugo praises him through the goldsmith's art.' At the bottom of the book cover, Hugo represents himself offering the very book he has decorated to St Nicolas, patron saint of the priory of Oignies.

The glorification of Christ through munificence is epitomized in late-medieval representations of the adoration of the Magi, which typically show gold and silver objects in the latest artistic styles being offered to the infant Christ. Although such objects are invariably secular, they set a clear precedent for the practice of worshipping Christ with gifts. It is fitting that the relics of the three kings should have been preserved in the largest reliquary shrine to survive from the Middle Ages, the magnificent *Three Kings Shrine* in Cologne Cathedral. Not only was the shrine itself conceived as a royal gift to Christ – behind the three kings, represented in an Adoration at one end of the shrine, the patron Emperor Otto IV, inscribed 'REX', is shown holding a reliquary casket as if he were a fourth king – but it also became a powerful focus for the pious donations of pilgrims.

While the emotive and symbolic potential of the arts was exploited throughout the Middle Ages, it had its detractors. St Bernard of Clairvaux (d.1153), founder of the Cistercian Order, decried the extravagance of decorating churches. Proto-reformers such as the Lollards and John Wycliffe condemned the opulent self-indulgence of the clergy and its exploitation of the superstitious populace. In northern Europe and England this came to a head with the Protestant Reformation, which called for a more personal and direct approach to salvation. The reformers condemned the intoxicating and distracting details of church ritual together with the vast numbers of glittering artefacts that were needed to sustain it.

The filigree finials for the Scroll of the Law and the silver and gilt wire and fringe of the Torah Mantle emphasize the beauty of worship.

Women from privileged backgrounds have always been in constant contact with silver. Silver was used in jewellery and silver lace, in needlework tools, in tea-making utensils, in the extensive toilet services that adorned their dressing-tables, not to mention the household plate. Although women might have enjoyed the use of lavish quantities of family plate, goldsmiths' records show that women were seldom the purchasers of silver and they owned very little in their own right. If a woman outlived her husband, most of the family silver passed to their eldest son as part of the estate. In the unusual cases where a woman did choose and purchase silver items of her own, the heraldic convention of using a lozenge-shaped cartouche for a woman's crest has often allowed us to identify her.

Women were actively engaged in many aspects of the silver trade, and some undertook formal apprenticeships through the Goldsmiths' Company.

The toilet service was usually the grandest of the silver items used particularly by women, and was intended as much for semi-public display as for its purpose in dressing. A disproportionate number have survived, often as part of the furnishings of a state bedchamber, as at Chatsworth.

However, they usually worked within family businesses so their contribution remains largely hidden. The small number of women who registered a maker's mark were often prompted to do so by the death of their husbands – Hester Bateman, Elizabeth Godfrey and Anne Tanqueray were among those who maintained flourishing businesses in their own names as widows. Many adopted a maker's mark shaped like the woman's lozenge used in heraldry.

Among the anonymous artisans who supplied the retailers, women often specialized in finishing, burnishing or chasing. Many were also engaged in the making of silver lace, buttons and buckles. Small unmarked silver goods and trinkets, many made by women, were sold through toyshops such as the famous one kept by Mrs Chevenix. When she sold the lease of Strawberry Hill House to Horace Walpole, he joked that it was 'a little plaything that I got out of Mrs Chevenix shop'.

According to Chambers's *Cyclopaedia* (1795),'The dressing-boxes, wherein are kept the paints, pomatums, essences, patches &c., the pincushion, powder box, brushes &c. are esteemed parts of the equipage of a lady's toilet.' These examples are flatchased with the Persian and Chinese motifs fashionable in the 1680s.

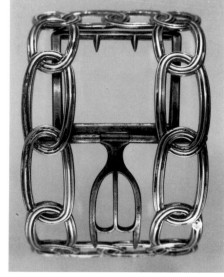

Above: Matthew Boulton attributed Birmingham's industrial success to the popularity of two dress accessories: buckles and buttons. Elaborate shoe-buckles were in fashion for both women and men during most of the 18th century. They were made from cut steel and paste (imitation gemstones) as well as silver.

Above: Botanical imagery was popular throughout Europe in the 17th century, influenced by the introduction of new species of exotic plants. Tulips and daffodils of embossed silver are applied to the filigree cover of this mid-17th-century pocket-sized mirror.

Right: Women were the principal consumers of silver lace, which was woven from threads of silk encased in flattened silver wire by craftsmen called orrice-weavers. When the lace, which was sold by weight, became tarnished or worn it was burnt and the silver recycled.

Below: Practical accessories such as sewing tools were made for the wealthy in silver and silvergilt. This early 18th-century case has separate compartments for the thimble and the needles, and would have hung from a lady's waist on a chatelaine.

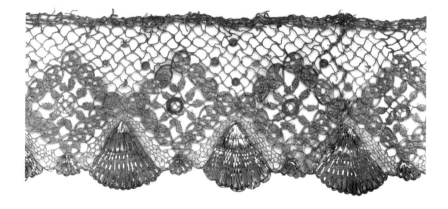

Right: This teacup of about 1710 can be identified as the property of a woman from the lozenge-shaped cartouche around the armorials. Tea was expensive, and it was usually the lady of the house who presided over its serving, accompanied by fine caddies, teapots and teacups of silver or imported porcelain.

SILVER IN PAINTINGS

The weights, key to a strong box and coins refer to the assay master's profession.

The value of silver, the high status enjoyed by craftsmen, the involvement of artists in design and the
wealth of owners have ensured the frequent depiction
of silver in paintings since the medieval period. Other
reasons for illustrating the production and consumption
of silver were demands for a visual record of authorship
or ownership and the many symbolic meanings associated with silver. Silver represented earthly authority,
reward or ritual; it also suggested luxury and excess, a
world in which material pleasures decisively
outweighed spiritual concerns. Whatever the underlying significance of its portrayal, to render convincingly
the sensuous surface appeal of silver was always a challenge to an artist's virtuoso skills.

Among the earliest images of the production of silver are the fifteenth-century manuscript illuminations (Nationalbibliothek, Vienna) of silver mining at Kutna Hora in Bohemia, where the richest silver mines in Europe had been discovered in the thirteenth century. The guild chapels of the town's magnificent cathedral dedicated to St Barbara, patron saint of miners, are also decorated with fifteenth-century frescoes showing miners and minters at work. Goldsmiths' guilds were responsible for commissioning the earliest pictures of goldsmiths at work, in the form of St Eligius and St Dunstan, their patron saints. The painting of St Eligius executed by Petrus Christus in 1449 (Lehman Collection of the Metropolitan Museum of Art, New York) was probably commissioned by the goldsmiths' guild of Antwerp. It depicts the saint selling a ring to a richly dressed couple, surrounded by precious raw materials and a goldsmith's stock-in-trade, which include silver flagons, coconut and crystal mounted cups, rings and other pieces of jewellery.

It is a short step from sacred portraits to those of actual goldsmiths. The earliest date from fifteenth-century Netherlands: in 1436 Jan van Eyck painted John de Leeuw, dean of the goldsmiths' guild of Bruges, holding a ring (Kunthistorisches Museum, Vienna). The connection between artist and goldsmith was close for both ultimately depended on skill in *disegno*, which manifests itself in meticulous drawing and engraving. Significantly, both Martin Schongauer and Albrecht Dürer were the sons of goldsmiths and could turn their hands to designing elaborate pieces of tableware and jewellery. In 1486, at the end of his apprenticeship to his father, Dürer drew him holding a statuette of a flagbearer, presumably of his own making (Graphische Sammlung Albertina, Vienna). By the mid-sixteenth century the spread of humanism boosted the claims of leading goldsmiths and artists to theoretical knowledge as well as craftsmanship. The Nuremberg goldsmith Wenzel Jamnitzer was portrayed in the 1560s (Musée d'Art et d'Histoire, Geneva) holding tools he had invented, a proportion compass and the converting rule for the specific gravity of the metals. The vase in the niche is also a Jamnitzer

The austere dress of the old miser contrasts with her lavish jewels and plate.

creation, for he specialized in finely wrought gold vases containing silver flowers. He establishes his authorship of the silver figure of Neptune on the table before him by pointing to the drawing for it.

Among the Nuremberg patricians and merchants portrayed by Nicolas Neufchâtel are an assay master and his wife weighing a silver covered goblet. The painting is reminiscent of the portraits of goldsmith bankers and their wives produced in great numbers in Antwerp from around 1525. But the later images are clearly didactic, reflecting contemporary debates on the morality of usury and profit, and warning against the accumulation of worldly goods at the expense of spiritual life. In Quentin Metsys's prototype for this genre the balance is more or less maintained, for the wife watches intently while turning the pages of her prayer book as her husband weighs the coins and luxury goods in front of him (Musée du Louvre, Paris). This injunction to godly behaviour was turned into a

The flare on Revere's burnished teapot is echoed in multiple reflections of flesh, tools and linen.

condemnation of avarice in later variations. The market for such salutary works was evidently alive 100 years later when Hendrick Gerritz. Pot painted an old woman miser.

By the early seventeenth century, however, silver was more frequently used in paintings to give form to the vanitas allegory: 'Vanity, vanity all is vanity,' a citation from Ecclesiastes 1: 2 commented on the fleeting nature of life on earth and the futility of human endeavours. The earliest instance of an independent vanitas still-life seems to be a painting by Jacques de Gheyn dated 1603 (Metropolitan Museum of Art, New York), which comprises simply a skull and soap bubble in a niche, with coins on the ledge before them. But the vanitas paintings of the Madrid artist Antonio de Pereda were conceived on an ambitiously Baroque scale, with angels presiding over a cornucopia of earthly riches and emblems of power.

Not every seventeenth-century painting containing silver intended to make a moral point. Silver had long been associated with nobility and kingship, symbolizing legitimate authority, ritual and riches, a tradition manifest even in religious paintings depicting the gifts of the Magi or the Magdalene's ointment jar. In 1624 Juan Bautista de Espinosa painted an opulent buffet representing the *modus vivendi* of a noble Spanish household (Masaveu Collection, Spain), while in the new Dutch republic artists like Pieter Claesz. and Willem Claesz. Heda painted both vanitas works and monochrome breakfast still-lifes that reflect no more than the artist's virtuoso skills. Although profligacy was deplored by ministers and moralists, communal feasting with a heavy emphasis on collective ritual was an important part of civic life. Standing salts, ewers, basins and goblets served as inanimate witnesses to such occasions and were painted both for their commemorative and decorative effect. Abraham van Beyeren and Willem Kalf above all are associated with the painting of these *pronkstilleven*, the lavish displays of costly tableware and succulent delicacies that were brought to Restoration England by Pieter van Roestraten. His meticulous still-life compositions included highly fashionable pieces – notably wine coolers and incense burners – in the collections of individual patrons. But they were also intended as celebrations of nature and art, demonstrating the artist's delight in *trompe l'œil* effects, possibly as part of larger decorative schemes.

Roestraten was among the first artists to treat the paraphernalia of tea-making as a still-life subject in itself. But depictions of the fashionable social ritual of tea-drinking, which brought silver off the buffet and banqueting table into the heart of respectable family life, appeared in Britain around 1720. The transformation of the risqué 'merry company' genre into the decorous conversation piece first accomplished by Franco-Flemish artists like Joseph van Aken was swiftly adopted by British artists to portray upper- and middle-class families at home around the tea table. Apprenticed to an engraver to the silver trade, William Hogarth was especially well placed to accessorize his group portraits with the latest styles in tea wares. But

Hogarth also understood the older symbolic meanings attached to silver. For example, the Rococo pierced silver fruit basket in *The Graham Children* is as much a vanitas reference as the cupid bearing Time's scythe on top of the clock or the cat eyeing the caged bird. Above all, Hogarth's modern moral painting cycles revived silver's association with greed and excess. In *The Rake's Progress*, Rakewell inherits a chest of gold and silver from his miser father, while his own decadence is symbolized by the silver racing trophy he wins at Epsom for his horse Silly Tom and the platter proffered during his drunken feasting at the Rose Tavern in Drury Lane, on which the posture dancer is about to perform. Similarly, in *Marriage à la mode*, the Countess's extravagant silver toilet service was an ostentatious status symbol but undoubtedly carried vanitas connotations as well. In the final scene, the table is a wicked parody of a Heda or Claesz. breakfast-piece: a large two-handled cup is set out on a dirty tablecloth, accompanied by a meagre boiled egg and a pig's head that is about to be seized by a starving dog.

Hogarth was probably the last artist to have a contemporary audience able to understand the meanings associated with silver. As silver became a widespread commodity it lost its exclusive cachet and with it disappeared the desire to celebrate in painting its manufacture, possession or usage, still less its conflation with gross materialism. Moreover, the increasingly availability of illustrated trade handbooks and technical treatises, drawings and engraved designs, as well as the growing tendency to use subcontractors and specialist suppliers, undermined the concept of the individual creativity of the working goldsmith. Significantly, the last painting to commemorate this role was produced at some distance from the most advanced tendencies of the trade. The Boston patriot Paul Revere was depicted in the late 1760s by John Singleton Copley as a craftsman in shirt and waistcoat, musing on the engraving he was about to apply to a silver teapot of his own making.

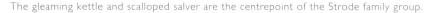

The gleaming kettle and scalloped salver are the centrepoint of the Strode family group.

CAPTIONS AND CREDITS

All objects are silver unless stated otherwise. Accession numbers are sited for objects from the V&A's collection.

Key to abbreviations (for objects in the V&A)

AAD	Archive of Art and Design
C	Ceramics
d, h, l	diameter, height, length
FE	Far Eastern Collection
M	Metalwork, Silver and Jewellery
NAL	National Art Library
PDP	Prints, Drawings and Paintings Collection

INTRODUCTION 7–11

Page from Jewel House issue book, 1768: Public Record Office (LC9/45)
Engraving of a milkmaid on Mayday: *Laitiere de Mai* from *Mémoires et observations faites par un voyageur en Angleterre*, 1698, Museum of London
Touchneedles and suspension bracket: needles are copper tipped with gold of varying alloys; pierced suspension bracket is silver, Spanish, dated 1682, unmarked. L: 51cm. (M.49-1971)
Brooch: *Seraph*, designed and made by Kevin Coates, silver, gold, titanium and opal, English 1989 (M.16-1996)

Section I: Design and Context

MEDIEVAL 12–15

Mérode Cup: silvergilt with *plique-à-jour* enamel panels, probably made in Flanders *c*.1400. H: 17.5cm. (403-1872)
The Last Supper: plaque decorated with translucent enamel, French *c*.1350. 31 x 80mm. Copyright British Museum
Pusey Horn: mounted in silvergilt, English *c*.1400. H: 25.25cm. (M.220-1938)

PLATE AND PIETY 16–17

Life of St Edmund: John Lydgate (d. *c*.1451), paint on vellum, English 1434. H: 6cm. By permission of the British Library (Harley MS.2278 f.4v)
Gloucester Candlestick: Gilt, base metal, English *c*.1107–13. H: 51.2cm. (7649-1861)
Diptych: silvergilt and translucent enamel, English *c*.1340. H: 4.1cm. (M.544-1910)
Christiaan de Hondt, Abbot of Ter Duingen: *c*.1499, oil on panel, Belgian. H: 30cm. Royal Museum of Fine Art, Antwerp
Hand reliquary: silver parcel-gilt, Flemish *c*.1450. H: 22.8cm. (M.353-1956)
Chalice: silvergilt, English *c*.1160. H: 14.2cm. Canterbury Cathedral

THE RENAISSANCE 18–21

The Feast of Ahaseurus and Esther: H. von der Heide, Lübeck *c*.1500–10, oil on panel. Museum für Kunst unt Kulturgeschichte der Hansestadt Lübeck
Dish: silvergilt, Portuguese, early 16th century, embossed with scenes from the Siege of Troy, engraved arms of Pinto e Cunha. D: 30 cm. (M.2-1938)
Burghley Nef: nautilus shell mounted in silver parcel-gilt, Paris 1527–8, mark of Pierre le Flamand. H. 34cm. (M.40-1959)

SPOONS: THE UNIVERSAL LUXURY 22–23

Fork: London 1632–3, mark of Richard Crosse, engraved crest of John Manners. L: 18.5cm. (M.358-1923)
Les femmes à table en l'absence de leurs maris: Abraham Bosse, print, Paris 1637 (PDP, 29534B)
Two Tichborne Spoons from a set of 12: silvergilt, London 1592–3. Hampshire County Museum Service, Winchester
Monkey Spoon: painted enamel on silver, Franco-Flemish mid-15th century. L: 24.1cm. (C.2-1935)
Strickland Spoon: York 1668–9, mark of Thomas Mangy, engraved crest of Strickland of Boynton. L: 20.5cm. (M.12-1932)
Three early spoons: right to left, diamond point: London 1493–4, mark a fish. L: 16cm. (1947-1900); wodewose: London, 15th century, mark of Deryk Knyff. L: 20.25cm. (M.65-1921); Rouen spoon: Rouen, early 14th century, mark an Agnus Dei in a circle. L: 16.6cm. (110-1865)
Travelling set: silvergilt, London *c*.1690, mark TT below a coronet. H. of beaker: 8cm. (M.62-c-1949)

MANNERISM 24–27

Solomon and the Treasure of the Temple: Frans Franken II, oil on canvas, Antwerp 1633. Louvre, Paris
Lomellini Ewer and Basin: Genoa 1621–2, mark of Giovanni Aelbosco, arms of Giacomo Lomellini. H. of ewer: 53.5cm, d. of basin: 64cm. (M.11-1974)
Design for a ewer: Cornelius Floris, based on designs by Enea Vico, engraving published Antwerp 1548 (PDP, 27699)

CHARLES I AS PATRON 28–29

Charles I, Queen Henrietta Maria and Charles Prince of Wales, Dining in Public (detail): Gerrit Houckgeest, oil on canvas, 1635. 63.2 x 92.4cm. The Royal Collection, H M Queen Elizabeth II
Group of three counter boxes and one flat box: counter boxes English, mid-17th century, no hallmarks (V&A 708-1868, 790-1891, M.316-1921; flat box mark WP in a rectangle (6767-1860)
Lord Keeper's Cup: silvergilt, London 1626–7, mark unidentified RB mullet below. H: 70cm. (M.59(1-2)-1993)
Sketch for a basin, of The Birth of Venus: Peter Paul Rubens, black chalk and oil on canvas, *c*.1630. The National Gallery, London
Dolphin Basin: London, dated 1635, signed by Christian van Vianen, unmarked. H: 48.5cm. (M.1-1918)

WELCOME AND BATH CUPS 30–31

The city architect Wolf Jacob Stromer offering the Wilkomm at the innauguration of the Schloss Kirchensittenbach: illustration from the *Wilkomm Buch von Kirchensittenbach*, Nuremberg 1593, Germanisches Nationalmuseum
Tazza: silvergilt, Zurich *c*.1675, mark of Hans Rudolph Boller. H: 23.8cm. (627-1872)
Roman Bath: Johann Theodor de Bry, engraving for a tazza bowl, Netherlandish *c*.1600 (PDP, 28356)
Half of a double cup: silvergilt, bowl and stem Nuremberg *c*.1590, mark of Hans Petzold, the foot Augsburg, mark of Christoph Lencker. H: 18.8cm. (485-1873). The other half of this cup is in the Österreichisches Museum für Angewandte Kunst, Vienna
Grünehagener Brotherhood Standing Cup and Cover: silvergilt, Hanover 1717, mark of Carl Junge. H: 57.5cm. (116-1864)
Design for a wager cup: Paul Flindt, engraving, Nuremberg *c*.1600 (PDP, E.2678-1910)

BAROQUE 32–35

Tankard: parcel-gilt, London *c*.1670, mark of Jacob Bodendick, arms of Henry St John. H: 23.5cm. Private collection
Papal mace: parcel-gilt, Rome 1696–1710, mark of Giovanni Giardini da Forli, arms of Pope Benedict XIV, shield and initials of Pope Pius VII. H: 101.5cm. (646-1906)
Frame: silvergilt, Paris 1672–7, unmarked. H: 30.9cm. (738-1882)

THE NEW DRINKS 36–37

Coffee urn: Amsterdam 1714, mark unidentified OA crowned. H: 33cm. (561(1-2)-1907)
Chocolate cup: silvergilt, London *c*.1690–5, unidentified mark FS/S crowned. H: 11.5cm. (M.6(1-3)-1992)
Tea kettle and stand: London *c*.1727–37, mark of Charles Frederick Kandler. H: 34.25cm. (M.49(1-3)-1939)
A Tea Party: Josef van Aken, about 1720, oil on canvas, 37.4 x 45.7cm. Manchester City Art Galleries
A Cavalier and a Woman Drinking Chocolate: dressed print, French, late 17th century. Pierpont Morgan Library, New York
Teapot: London 1705–6, mark of Simon Pantin, engraved arms of Plomer. H: 21.5cm. (172-1919)

THE ARRIVAL OF THE DINNER SERVICE 38–41

Chesterfield Wine Cooler: London 1727–8, mark of Paul Crespin overstriking Paul de Lamerie. H: 26.5cm. (M.1-1990). The pair to this is in the National Museums of Scotland, Edinburgh
A Table of Fifteen or Sixteen Covers for a Supper: engraving from Vincent La Chapelle's *The Modern Cook*, vol. I, 2nd edition, 1736. The Brotherton Library, University of Leeds
Dessin d'un Pot à Oille: Nicolas-Ambroise Cousinet, pencil and ink drawing, *c*.1690. Nationalmuseum Stockholm

LAYING THE TABLE 42–43

A Fashionable Table: Pieter Angellis, oil on canvas, *c*.1720–30. Courtesy of Ackermann & Johnson
Knife box: Mahogany veneer with silver mount, containing silver flatware, London around 1770–80 (W.65-1950)

Caster: one of a set of three, London 1689–90, mark RH. H: 17.5cm. (M.39-1994)
Fish Trowel: London 1770–1, mark of Thomas Nash. L: 28.5cm. (647-1898)
Scallop Shell: London 1749–50, mark of Edward Aldridge. L: 13.5cm. (M.106-1940)
Tureen: London 1757–8, mark WI. H: 26cm. (V&A loan)
Sauceboat: probably designed by Nicolas Sprimont, English *c*.1745. 17.3cm. (M.41-1993)

REDISCOVERY OF THE ANTIQUE 44–47

Pair of Sauceboats: London 1773–4, mark of John Carter after designs by Robert Adam. H: 13.7cm. (M.13&a-1987)
Matthew Boulton's factory at Soho, Birmingham: print *c*.1781. Birmingham City Archives (MPB/342)

ARMS 48–49

Designs for sword hilts: Jeremias Wachsmutl, Augsburg *c*.1750 (PDP, 24342-2)
Small-sword: three-coloured gold hilt, German *c*.1760 (M.40-1973)
Rapier: English *c*.1640, mark TH monogram (M.2724-1931)
Small-sword: silver hilt, London 1676–7, unidentified mark WB conjoined (M.153-1937)
Small-sword: silver hilt with agate grip, England *c*.1730 (M.155-1922)
Detail of small-sword hilt: see M.153-1937
Flintlock pistol: one of a pair, Dublin *c*.1770, lock signed by Thomas Trulock (M.144-1929)

REGENCY AND EMPIRE 50–53

Regency Fete or John Bull in the Conservatory: print, 28 June 1911. Courtesy of the Print Collection, Lewis Walpole Library, Yale University
Hot water urn: silvergilt and ebony, Paris 1798–1809, mark of Jean-Baptiste Claude Odiot. H: 43cm. (M.3-c-1973)
Section of the Portuguese Service (Baixela da Victoria): designed by Domingos António de Sequeira, silver parcel-gilt, Lisbon, 1813–16 (V&A Wellington Museum, Apsley House)

THE DISPERSAL OF HISTORIC PLATE 54–55

The Plumb Pudding in Danger or State Epicures taking un Petit Souper: James Gillray, coloured engraving, 1805 (PDP, 15454)
Illustration of objects from William Beckford's collection at Fonthill: from John Rutter's *Delineations of Fonthill and its Abbey*, 1823 (NAL 63.B.85)
Ewer and basin: silvergilt, probably Paris *c*.1580, unmarked, chased scenes based on designs by Etienne Delaunay. H. of ewer: 29.2cm, d. of basin: 52.1cm. (V&A loan)
Ewer: silver parcel-gilt, probably Swiss, early 15th century, unmarked. H: 29cm. (7914-1862)
Tankard: parcel-gilt set with Swedish, Danish, French, German and English coins, Arboga, Sweden 1727–35, mark of Johann Dragman. H: 20 cm. (864-1882)
Aldobrandini Tazza: silvergilt, the foot probably Spanish, the bowl possibly Flemish, *c*.1575, unmarked, with the figure of the Emperor Domitian and the arms of Cardinal Ippolito Aldobrandini, later Pope Clement VII. H: 41.3cm. (M.247-1956)

ECLECTICISM 56–59

Tureen: after a design by Karl Friedrich Schinkel, Berlin 1842–7, mark of Johann Georg Hossauer. H: 51cm. (M.34,1-3,1992)
Page from F. Knight's *Vases and Ornaments*: 1833 (NAL 58.A.57 pl.14)

ELKINGTON'S THE INNOVATORS 60–61

Newhall Street Factory, Birmingham: *Cornish Brothers Strangert's Guide through Birmingham and its Manufactories*, *c*.1855 (NAL 254.D)
Elkington's electroplating works showing plating dynamo and vats: from *Cassell's Illustrated Exhibitor*, 1852
Oval stamp of Science and Art Department (applied to all electrotypes produced under the Elkington-South Kensington Museum agreement): from the back of a V&A electrotype
Pair of electrotype lions *c*.1885: copied from the silver originals made c.1650 for the Danish king, Rosenborg Castle, Denmark. H: 93cm. (1885-194&a)
Coloured illustration of silver group: from J.B. Waring's *Masterpieces of the International Exhibition of 1862*, including the silver table designed by L. Morel-Ladeuil (NAL 49.D.20-22)
Designs for salt cellars: Elkington's third drawing book (AAD)
Card case: designed for Elkington's by George Stanton, electroplated nickel silver and parcel-gilt, 1852. L: 9.5cm. (1302-1854)

DESIGN REFORM IN ENGLAND 62–63

Medieval Court: *Views of the Great Exhibition*, 1851 (NAL)
Decanter stopper: designed by J.C. Horsely for the Summerly Art Manufactures in 1847, made by Smith & Nicholson, London 1855–6. H: 11.3cm. (795-1864)
Flagon: parcel-gilt, London 1850–1, mark of Charles and George Fox. H: 62cm. (2743-1851)
Milton Shield: designed by L. Morel Ladeuil for Elkington and Co., exhibited at the International Exhibition, Paris 1867. L: 88cm. (546-1868)
Centrepiece: designed by Sir George Hayter, London 1842, mark of Mortimer and Hunt. H: 99cm. Reproduced with kind permission of the Trustees of the Montefiore Endowment at Ramsgate (V&A loan)
Teapot and Cost Book: electroplated prototype designed by Christopher Dresser for James Dixon & Sons, design number 2275 with the original Cost Book, 1879. Phillips Fine Art auctioneers

THE DILEMMA OF THE 1890s: OLD OR NEW? 64–67

Door handle: one from a set of 15 designed by Georges de Feure, electroplated silver on copper, Paris *c*.1900. L: 20cm. (2-n-1901)
Martelé jug: Gorham & Co., U.S.A. c.1904. Private collection
Collection of flatware: parcel-gilt, mixed metals and enamel, American, 1880–90. Courtesy of Nicolas Harris

NOVELTIES 68–69

Henry Manton tradecard: about 1845. Birmingham Museums and Art Gallery
Front cover of WMF 1901 catalogue: *Württembergische Metallwarenfabrik*, Geislingen, Germany

Handpress operators in the piercing shop of J.W. Evans & Sons Ltd: photograph *c*.1901. J.W. Evans Sons Ltd
Illustration of sugar tongs: Art Journal Illustrated Catalogue: The Industry of all Nations, London 1851, p. 27 (NAL PP6B)
Collection of 19th and early 20th-century small wares: Neales Fine Art Auctioneers
Inkstand: London 1845–6, mark of Robert Hennell. D: 19.5cm. (325-e-1959)
Gypsy tea kettle and stand: London 1890, mark of Alfred Benson and Henry Hugh Webb. H: 57.5cm. Neales Fine Art Auctioneers

THE EMERGENCE OF MODERNISM 70–71

Decanter: designed by C.R. Ashbee, glass with silver mounts, the finial set with a chrysoprase, London 1904–5, mark of the Guild of Handicraft. H: 23.5. (M.121-1966)
Sea Beaker: designed by Richard Yorke Gleadowe CVO, engraved by George Friend, London 1933–4, marks of Henry George Murphy and the Falcon mark for Murphyís workshop. H: 10.8cm. (M.19-1991)
Tea and Coffee service: designed and made in the Jean Puiforçat workshop, ivory handles, rosewood tray, French *c*.1930–5. Gift of Mrs John David Eaton to the Royal Ontario Museum, Toronto
Tea Service: designed by H.G. Murphy, kingwood handles, London 1933–4. H. of teapot: 16cm. (M.6-b,-1985)
Cigarette Casket: silver inlaid with blue enamel, London 1923–4, mark of Harold Stabler. The Worshipful Company of Goldsmiths, London

THE IMPACT OF MODERNISM 72–75

Poster for 1938 exhibition at the Goldsmiths' Hall: designed by Edward McKnight Kauffer. The Worshipful Company of Goldsmiths, London
Tea and coffee service: designed and made by Christian Dell, walnut fittings, German *c*.1925. H. of coffeepot: 26.5cm. (257-262,-1970)
Cocktail set: designed by Keith Murray, made by Mappin & Webb, London *c*.1935, unmarked, contemporary photograph. The Worshipful Company of Goldsmiths, London.

THE POST-WAR REVIVAL 76–79

Tea service: designed by Robert Goodden, CBE, RDI, parcel-gilt, London 1950–1, Festival of Britain mark, mark of Leslie Durbin, inscribed with rhyming couplets composed by Robert Goodden. H. of teapot 18.5cm. (M.176-c,-1976; M.80-1982)
Tea and coffee service: designed by Kazumasa Yamashita, made by Officina Alessi spa, electroplate prototype for limited silver production, Italian 1983. H. of coffee pot: 22.5cm, l. of tray: 51cm. (M.59-e-1988)
Coffee pot: designed and made in the Sigurd Persson workshop, rosewood handle, Swedish 1992. H: 25.5cm. (M.13-1995)

INTERNATIONAL HIGHLIGHTS OF THE PAST TEN YEARS 80–81

The Entropy of Red: trumpet designed and made by Robert Baines, woven silver wire, lacquered red, Australian 1995. H: 40.4cm. (M.26-1996)
Butterfly Salt: made by Fred Rich for Garrards, silver, gold, enamel, London 1995. Courtesy of Fred Rich

Heat Haze vase: designed and made by Yukie Osumi, silver with lead and gold surface inlay, Japan 1992 (FE.561-1992)
Carafes and bowls: designed by Tobia and Afra Scarpa for the Studio of San Lorenzo, silvergilt interior, Italy 1990. Studio of San Lorenzo
Teapot: designed and made by Johannes Kuhnen, silver, anodized aluminium, stainless steel, Australia 1993

Section II: The Craft

WHAT IS A GOLDSMITH? 82–85

Portrait of Paul Crespin: anonymous, oil on canvas, English about 1720 (PDP, P.29-1985)
Goldsmiths' workshop: engraving by A. Guynet, 1646. Private collection
Portrait of John Lonyson: Steven van der Meulen, oil on panel, English 1565. The Worshipful Company of Goldsmiths
Engraving of women burnishers: from J. Tourgan's *Les Grandes Usines*, vol. I, 1868 (NAL 20.K)

WHAT IS A HALLMARK? 86–87

The Warden striking a mark on a plate assisted by his officer: detail from invitation to Goldsmiths' annual service, 1694. The Master and Fellows, Magdalene College, Cambridge (PL 2973/504d)
Chest of the Ulm Goldsmiths Guild: Ulm 1501, and later. Ulmer Museum, Germany
Signature of Charles Kandler: Largeworkers' Book for 1727. The Worshipful Company of Goldsmiths
Ghent markplate: names, marks and dates of the Goldsmiths Guild of Ghent, 1527–1617. Electrotype of Flemish origin (1876-15)
Band of hallmarks: date letter 'a' for 1678–9 (from a beaker, silver M.405-1927); lion passant for 1732–3, London mark – a crowned leopard's head for 1732–3, both from a tea caddy (M.1767-1944); detail of part-marks struck on the hinge of a shagreen box, mid-eighteenth century (V&A)
Underside of a caster showing overstruck mark and scratchweight: London 1754–5, mark of Elizabeth Godfrey overstriking the retailer. H: 15.25cm. (M.158-b-1939)

WORKING AND DECORATING SILVER 88–91

Photograph of a craftsman hammering out silver on a stake
Iron panel: The Story of Judith and Holofernes, damascened in gold and silver, Milan, mid-16th century. H: 23.25cm. (M.663-1910)
Chased plaque: England 1772, signed by Christopher Heckel. H: 9.7cm. (M.54,1-3,-1993)
Pair of dessert stands: silvergilt, London 1698–9, mark of Benjamin Pyne, engraved arms of Sir William Courtenay of Powderham Castle, Devon. D: 24cm (M.77&a-1947)

HOW TO CAST 92–93

Engraving of silver workshop showing casting, hammering out, raising and planishing: Denis Diderot's *Encyclopédie*, Paris 1776–7 (NAL 68.E)
Mould for a statuette of the Virgin and Child: bronze, German 17th century. L: 6.25cm. (M.97-1929)
Underside of two candlesticks: (left) London 1693–4, unidentified mark I.S overstriking another. D: 13.5cm (M.6-

1963); (right): London 1719–20, Britannia Standard, mark of John White. D: 10cm. (M.419a-1922)
Jug: silvergilt, English *c*.1750. H: 12.75cm. (M.248-1921)
Ewer: silvergilt, London 1700–1, Britannia Standard, mark of David Willaume, engraved arms of Richard Hill. H: 21cm. (822-1890)

CARE AND CLEANING 94–95

Ingrid Barré: at work in V&A Metalwork Conservation
Quotation from Jonathon Swift: *Directions to Servants in General*, London 1745
Mostyn Standing Salt: silvergilt, London 1586–7, unidentified mark T in a pearl-bordered shield. H: 41.5cm. (146–1886)
Nigel Blades: in the V&A Science Laboratory checking monitoring equipment
Islington Cup: in original case, parcel-gilt, London 1802–3, designed by John Thurston, modelled by Edmund Coffin, bearing mark of Joseph Preedy, inscription engraved by John Roper. H. of cup 49cm. (M.12-b-1987)

DESIGN 96–99

Mercury (detail): Baccio Baldini, engraving, Italian, 15th century, 3.24 x 2.20cm. Copyright British Museum (H.I.82.A.III.6.a.1)
Goldsmiths' tools falling from heaven: Christopher Jamnitzer, drawing (PDP, E.2357-1928)
Designs for ornament on plate: C. de Moelder, engraving, London 1694 (PDP, E.385-1926)

IMITATIONS AND SUBSTITUTES 100–101

Electrotype dish: Electrotype (1898–66) of Spanish, late 15th century original (147-1882)
Detail of reverse of 1898–66
Paktong candlestick: paktong, English *c*.1780. H: 26.5cm. (M.1092-1926)
Sauce tureen and stand: Sheffield Plate, English *c*.1780, engraved arms of Sir John Blunden. H: 19cm. (M.338-1922)
Oval dish: silvered brass, German, first half 18th century. L: 49.5cm. (1731-1892)
Jug with imitation hallmarks: brass, English *c*.1750. H: 11.25cm. (M.1050-1926)

SELLING SILVER 102–105

Interior of a Dutch goldsmith's shop: anonymous, Dutch, late 17th century. Premsela and Hamburger, Amsterdam.
Phillips Garden tradecard: London, *c*.1750. Copyright British Museum
Exterior of Mappin Brothers' shop, Regent Street: *Illustrated Times*, 31 May 1862 p.81 (NAL)
Hall's Library: 4 June 1789, J.Hall and I.Malton. Copyright British Museum

A LONDON BUSINESS 106–107

The Strand from the corner of Villiers Street: George Scharf, watercolour over pencil with ink, 1824. Copyright British Museum
Second tradecard of John Parker and Edward Wakelin: 1761. Westminster City Archives
Overstruck marks: Sheffield. 1774–5
Stanton Harcourt tableware: London 1768–9, mark of Parker

& Wakelin; ladles: London 1768–9, mark of Philip Norman, retailed by Parker & Wakelin. Courtesy of Sotheby's
Tea tub: London *c*.1768, mark of Parker and Wakelin. H: 10.9cm. (V&A loan)
Page from Parker & Wakelin's Workmen's Ledger Accounts (detail): Edward Wakelin, 27 August 1770 (AAD)

Section III: Attitudes to Silver

GIFTS, PRIZES AND REWARDS 108–111

Ewer and Basin: London 1705–6, Britannia Standard, mark of Philip Rollos, engraved arms of Queen Anne. H: of ewer: 32.5cm (M.23&a-1963)
Bowes Gold Cup: London 1675–6, mark of Jacob Bodendick, engraved with the arms of Sir William Bowes and Elizabeth Blakiston. H: 14.75cm. (M.63-1993)
Doncaster Cup: designed by H.H. Armstead for C.F. Hancock, silver partly oxydised, London 1857. H: 76cm on plinth. (M.65-b-1990)

THE GOLDSMITHS' COMPANY OF LONDON 112–113
(the following objects all belong to the Worshipful Company of Goldsmiths)
Goldsmiths' Hall: unknown artist, watercolour, 1835, 91.5 x 60cm
Bowes Cup: silvergilt, 1554, unidentified mark of a queen's head. H: 49cm
Amity Cup: Kevin Coates, silvergilt and oxidised silver set with a pearl, 1982. H: 14.5cm
Vase on the theme of a jay's wing: Jane Short, silver and enamel, 1990. H: 20cm
Water jug: Shannon O'Neill, silver, 1995. H: 32.5cm
Three part necklace: Wendy Ramshaw, 18ct. gold, black enamel and black basalt, 1984. L: 50cm

COLLECTING 114–117

Exhibition of Works of Art at Ironmongers' Hall: *Illustrated London News*, 18 May 1861, p.474 (NAL)
Vase and cover: Chinese porcelain with silvergilt mounts, probably London *c*.1665, mark of Wolfgang Howzer. H: 30.5cm. (M.308-1962)
Two-handled cup and Nautilus cup: Pieter van Roestraten, oil on canvas, Dutch, late 17th century, 74.5 x 63cm (PDP, P.4.1939)

FAKES, FORGERIES AND CONFECTIONS 118–119

Madonna and Child: silvergilt, French, 19th century. H: 21.5cm. (1198-1864)
Three counterfeit trifid-end spoons: Worshipful Company of Goldsmiths
Two designs for mounts of drinking horns: Reinhold Vasters of Aachen (PDP)
Stoneware jug with silvergilt mounts: mounts; London 1556–7, unidentified mark WC over a pig/grasshopper. H: 28cm. (215-1869)
Detail of hallmarks: Private collection
Two handled cup: English. H: 11cm. (M.323-1923)

SMALL SILVER FOR COLLECTORS 120–121

By Order of the Court: Alexander Stanhope Forbes, 1890, oil

on canvas, 152.5cm x 204.5cm. The Board of Trustees of the National Museums & Galleries on Merseyside, Walker Art Gallery
Line drawing of London hallmarks: *The Connoisseur*, vol. I, Sept.–Dec. 1901, p.11 (NAL)
Vinaigrette: gold and silvergilt, Dutch *c*.1800. H: 3.5cm. (M.64-1959)
Bottle tickets: Hungary Water, silvergilt, London 1826–7, mark of C Rawlings. D: 5cm (M.595-1944); Ketchup, England *c*.1790, no marks. D: 1.75cm (M.703-1944); White, English (Newcastle?), late 18th century, mark of J. Kirkup? D: 5cm (M.703-1944); Claret, Dublin *c*.1780, mark of B. Taitt. D: 5cm. (M.489-1944)
Tobacco box in the form of Nelson's death mask: silvergilt, English, early 19th century. L: 8.75cm. (835-1890)
Drinking Like a Fish Cup: London 1995, mark of Sarah Jones, with kind permission of Sarah Jones

CEREMONY AND AUTHORITY 122–125

Mace Bearer: detail from *The Coronation of James II*, Sandford 1687. Society of Antiquaries
The Three Kings Shrine: set with silver, gold, and gems, German 1170–1230. L: 180cm. Cologne Cathedral
Torah Mantle and Rimmonim: Mantle: silk velvet and silver brocade, Amsterdam 1650–1700. L: 114.5cm (349-1870 Textiles); Rimmonim: silver filigree, Italian (?) 17th century. H: 43cm. (350&a-1870)

WOMEN AND SILVER 126–127

Mariage à la Mode: The Countess's Morning Levée (detail): William Hogarth, oil on canvas, English, early 18th century. The National Gallery, London
Part of the Sizergh Toilet Service: London *c*.1680, mark of Robert Smythier. H: 15.8cm. (M.21-1968)
Mirror cover: possibly Dutch, mid-17th century, unmarked. H: 8.3cm. (537-1902)
Shoe buckle: London, late 18th century, mark SC perhaps for Samuel Cooke (M.31-1909)
Silver bobbin lace: English or French, mid-18th century. H: 13.5cm. (T.147-1984)
Thimble and needle case: silvergilt English, early 18th century, unmarked. L: 9.25cm. (813-1864)
Teacup: English *c*.1710, unmarked. H: 4.9cm. (M230-1930)

SILVER IN PAINTINGS 128–131

Assay Master and his Wife: attributed to Nicolas Neufchâtel, oil on panel, Nuremberg *c*.1561–7. H: 93.3 x 102.5cm. Christie's Images
The Miser: Hendrik Gerritsz, oil on canvas, Haarlem 1622, 104 x 82.5cm. Rheinisches Landesmuseum, Bonn
Paul Revere: John Singleton Copley, oil on canvas, U.S.A. 1768, 88.9 x 72.3cm. Gift of Joseph W. Revere, William B. Revere and Edward H.R. Revere. Courtesy Museum of Fine Arts, Boston
The Strode Family: William Hogarth, oil on canvas, English *c*.1738, 87 x 91.1cm. Tate Gallery, London

SELECTED FURTHER READING

General works

Blair, C. (ed.), *The History of Silver*, London, 1987
Clayton, M., *The Collector's Dictionary of the Silver and Gold in Great Britain and North America*, Woodbridge, 1985
Glanville, P., *Silver in England*, London, 1987
Gruber, A., *Silverware*, New York, 1985
Hernmarck, C., *The Art of the European Silversmith 1430–1830*, London, 1977
Oman, C., *English Domestic Silver*, London, 1934 and later editions
Truman, C. (ed), *Sotheby's Concise Encyclopedia of Silver*, London, 1993

Exhibition catalogues

Alexander, J.J.G., Binski, P., *The Age of Chivalry: Art in Plantagenet England, 1200–1400*, Royal Academy, London, 1985
Baker, M., Schroder, T. and Clowes, E.L., *Beckford and Hamilton Silver from Brodick Castle*, London, 1980
Baumstark, R., Seling, H., Seelig, L., Ulli, A., *Silber und Gold, Augsburger Goldschmiedekunst für die Höfe Europas*, Bayerisches National Museum, Munich, 1994
Bazzo, E. (ed) 1970–1995, *The Work of the Silversmith's Studio, San Lorenzo, Milan, 1995–96*, Victoria and Albert Museum, London, 1995–96
Birmingham City Museum, *Omar Ramsden 1873–1939, Centenary Exhibition of Silver*, Birmingham, 1973
Birmingham Gold and Silver 1773–1973, Birmingham, 1973
Bott, G., Pechstein, K., *Wenzel Jamnitzer und die Nürnberger Goldschmiedekunst 1500–1700*, Germanisches Nationalmuseum, Nuremberg, 1985
Brown, P., *Pyramids of Pleasure*, Fairfax House, York, 1990
The Keeping of Christmas, 1760–1840, Fairfax House, York, 1993
In Praise of Hot Liquors, Fairfax House, York, 1995
Christie's, *Glory of the Goldsmith (Treasures from the Al-Tajir Collection)*, London, 1989
Culme, J., *English Silver Treasures from the Kremlin*, Sotheby's, London, 1991
Davis, J.D., *The Genius of Irish Silver: A Texas Private Collection*, Colonial Williamsburg, 1991
Crighton, R.A., *Cambridge Plate*, Fitzwilliam Museum, Cambridge, 1975
Great Exhibition 1851, *Official Descriptive and Illustrated Catalogue of the Great Exhibition of the Works of Industry of all Nations*, London, 1851
Grosvenor Museum, *Chester Silver*, Chester, 1984
Hare, S., *Touching Gold and Silver*, Goldsmiths' Company, London, 1978
Paul de Lamerie, Goldsmiths' Company, London, 1990
Harrison, P., *Art and Design in Europe, 1800–1900*, Victoria and Albert Museum, London, 1987
Jones, M., *Fake: The Art of Deception*, British Museum, London, 1990

Kensington Palace, *A King's Feast: The Goldsmith's Art and Royal Banqueting in the 18th Century*, London, 1991
Lambert, S., *Pattern and Design: Designs for the Decorative Arts 1480–1980*, Victoria and Albert Museum, London, 1983
Metropolitan Museum of Art, *Gothic and Renaissance Art in Nuremberg 1300–1550*, New York and Nuremberg, 1986
Murdoch, T.V. *London Silver 1680 to 1780*, Museum of London, London, 1982
The Quiet Conquest: The Huguenots 1685 to 1985, Museum of London, London, 1985
Bayerisches Nationalmuseum *Modell und Ausführung in der Metallkunst*, Munich, 1989
Musée National de Versailles, Reunion des Musée National, *Versailles et les tables royales en Europe XVII–XIX siècles*, Paris, 1994
Museum Boymans – Van Beuningen *Silver of a New Era, International Highlights of Precious Metalware from 1880 to 1940*, Rotterdam, 1992
Queen's Gallery, Buckingham Palace, *Carlton House. Past Glories of George IV's Palace*, London, 1991–92
Sheffield City Museum, *Sheffield Silver 1773–1973*, Sheffield, 1973
Snodin, M., *Rococo Art and Design in Hogarth's England*, Victoria and Albert Museum, London, 1984
Tait, H., *Catalogue of the Waddesdon Bequest in the British Museum*, Vol II *The Silver Plate*, Vol III *The Curiosities*, London, 1988 and 1991
Ward, B.M. and G.W.R., *Silver in American Life*, New York, 1979
Venable, C. L., *Silver in America 1840–1940: A Century of Splendor*, Dallas Museum of Art, Dallas, 1994

Marks

Barrett. G.N., *Norwich Silver and its Marks 1565–1702*, Norwich, 1981
Boje, C.A., *Danske Sovmaerker*, Copenhagen, 1962
Citroen, K.A., *Amsterdam Silversmiths and their Marks*, Amsterdam, Oxford, New York, 1975
Crisp-Jones, R., *The Silversmiths of Birmingham and their Marks 1750–1980*, London, 1981
Culme, J., *Directory of Gold and Silversmiths, Jewellers and Allied Traders 1838–1914*, Woodbridge, 1987
Gill, M.A.V., *Marks of the Newcastle Goldsmiths 1702–1884*, Newcastle, 1974
A Directory of Newcastle Goldsmiths, Newcastle, 1980
Grimwade, A., *London Goldsmiths 1697–1837, their Marks and Lives*, London, 1976; revised edn, 1982
Helft, J., *Les Poinçons des provinces françaises*, Paris, 1968
Jackson, C.J., *English Goldsmiths and their Marks*, revised edn Woodbridge, 1989
Kent, T., *London Silver Spoonmakers 1500–1697*, London, 1981
Koonings, W., *Meestertekens van Nederlandse Goud en Zilversmeden 1850*, The Hague, 1963
Nocq, H., *Les Poinçons de Paris*, Vols I–IV, Paris, 1926

Rosenberg, M., *Der Goldschmiede Merkzeichen*, Vols I–III, Berlin, 1928

Sheffield, *The Sheffield Assay Office Register 1773–1907*, Sheffield, 1911

Tardy, *Les Poinçons de garantie internationaux pour l'argent*, Paris, 1977; English-language version, 1981

Special Subjects and Periods

Andren, E. and others, *Svenskt Silversmide 1520–1850*, Stockholm, 1963

Arminjon, C., *L'orfèvrerie au xixe siècle*, Paris, 1994

Babelon, J. and others *Les Grands Orfèvres de Louis XIII à Charles X*, Paris, 1965

Barr, E., *George Wickes 1698–1761: Royal Goldsmith*, London, 1980–83

Basle Historiches Museum, *The Historical Museum Basle, Guide to the Collections*, Basle, 1994

Bimenet-Privat, M., *Les Orfèvres Parisiens de la Renaissance 1506–1620*, Paris, 1992

Bradbury, F., *A History of Old Sheffield Plate*, Sheffield, 1912; reprinted 1968

Bury, S., *Victorian Electroplate*, London, 1971

Campbell, M., Gold, 'Silver and precious stones' in Blair, J., Ramsay, N. (eds) *English Medieval Industries*, London, 1991

Carrington, J.B., Hughes, G.R., *Plate of the Worshipful Company of Goldsmiths*, Oxford, 1926

Clark, G., *Symbols of Excellence: Precious Materials as Expressions of Status*, Cambridge, 1986

Crosby-Forbes, H.A., Kernan, J.D., Wilkins, R.S., *Chinese Export Silver 1785–1885* Milton, Mass., 1975

Culme, J., *Nineteenth-century Silver*, London, 1977

Davis, J.D., *English Silver at Williamsburg*, Colonial Williamsburg, 1976

Delaforce, A., Yorke, J., *Portugal's Silver Service*, Victoria and Albert Museum, London, 1992

Dennis, F., *Three Centuries of French Domestic Silver*, Metropolitan Museum of Art, New York, 1960

Dickinson, H.W., *Matthew Boulton*, Cambridge, 1937

Fales, M.G., *Early American Silver*, New York, 1970

Fritz, J.M., *Goldschmiedekunst der Gotik in Mitteleuropa*, Munich, 1982

Glanville, P., *Silver in Tudor and Early Stuart England*, Victoria and Albert Museum, London, 1989

Glanville, P., Faulds Goldsborough, J., *Women Silversmiths 1685–1845*, New York, 1990

Grimwade, A., *Rococo Silver 1727–1765*, London, 1974

Hayward, J.F., *Huguenot Silver in England 1688–1727*, London, 1959

Virtuoso Goldsmiths and the Triumph of Mannerism 1540–1620, London, 1976

Heal, A., *The London Goldsmiths 1200–1800*, London, 1935

Helliwell, S., *Collecting Small Silverware*, Oxford, 1988

Hughes, G., *Modern Silver Throughout the World*, London, 1967

Jewitt, L., Hope, W.StJ., *The Corporation Plate and Insignia of Office of the Cities and Towns of England and Wales*, W. StJohn Hope (ed), 1895

Kohlhausen, H., *Nürnberger Goldschmiedekunst des Mittelalters und der Dürerzeit, 1240 bis 1540*, Berlin, 1968

Krekel-Aalberse, A., *Art Nouveau and Art Deco Silver*, London, 1989

Lightbown, R., *Secular Goldsmiths' Work in Medieval France*, London, 1978

French Silver, (Catalogue of V&A collection) London, 1978

Catalogue of Scandinavian and Baltic Silver in the Victoria and Albert Museum, London, 1975

Lomax, J., *British Silver at Temple Newsam*, Leeds, 1992

Mabille, G., *Orfèvrerie française des XVI, XVII, XVIII siècles*, Paris, 1984

Metropolitan Museum of Art, *Highlights of the Untermyer Collection of English and Continental Decorative Arts*, New York, 1977

Mitchell, D. (Ed.), *Goldsmiths, Silversmiths and Bankers: Innovation and the Transfer of Skill, 1550–1750*, London, 1995

Molen, J.R.ter, *Van Vianen*, Utrecht, 1984

Moller, J.E.R., *Georg Jensen: The Danish Silversmith*, Copenhagen, 1985

Norfolk Museums, *Norwich Silver in the Collection of Norwich Castle Museum*, Norwich, 1981

Oman, C., *English Church Plate 597–1837*, London, 1957

Caroline Silver 1625–1688, London, 1970

English Engraved Silver, London, 1978

The English Silver in the Kremlin 1557–1663, London, 1961

The Golden Age of Hispanic Silver 1400–1665, London, 1968

Pechstein, K., *Goldschmiedewerke der Renaissance*, Kunstgewerbemuseum, Berlin 1971

Penzer, N.M., *The Book of the Wine Label*, London, 1947

Paul Storr, London, 1954; reprinted 1971

Pickford, I., *Silver Flatware, English, Irish and Scottish 1660–1980*, Woodbridge, 1983

Poliakoff, M., *Silver Toys and Miniatures*, London, 1986

Read, H. and Tonnochy, A., *Catalogue of Silver Plate: the Franks Bequest*, London, 1928

Rowe, R., *Adam Silver 1765–1795*, London, 1965

Scheffler, W., *Goldschmiede Niedersachsens*, Berlin and New York, 1965

Seelig, L., *Silver and Gold, Courtly Splendour from Augsburg*, Munich and New York, 1995

Seling, H., *Die Kunst der Augsburger Goldschmiede 1529–1860*, Vols I–IV, Munich, 1980, 1994

Schliemann, E. (ed.) *Die Goldschmiede Hamburgs*, Hamburg, 1985

Solodkoff, A. von, *Russian Gold and Silver*, London, 1981

Stancliffe, J., *Silver Bottle Tickets*, London, 1986

Theophilus, *On Divers Arts*, Smith, J.G. and C.S. (translation and eds), 2nd edn, 1979

Thornton, P., *Seventeenth-century Interior Decoration in England, France and Holland*, London, 1978

Authentic Decor 1620–1920, London, 1984

Untracht, Oppi, *Metal Techniques for Craftsmen*, 2nd edn, New York, 1975

Vickers, M. (ed), *Pots and Pans: A Colloquium on Precious Metals and Ceramics in the Muslim, Chinese and Graeco-Roman Worlds*, Oxford, 1985 and 1986

Warren, D.B., Howe, K.S., Brown, M.K., *Marks of Achievement: Four Centuries of American Presentation Silver*, Houston, 1987

Widman, D., *Sigurd Persson, en Mästare i Form*, 1994

Wilkinson, W.R.T., *Indian Colonial Silver*, London, 1973

Welch, R., *Hand and Machine*, London, 1986

MUSEUMS, GALLERIES, EXHIBITIONS

United Kingdom and Ireland

London

Bank of England Museum
Bank of England
Threadneedle Street EC2R 8AH

British Museum
Great Russell Street WC2R ORN

Courtauld Institute Galleries
Somerset House
The Strand WC2R ORN

Jewel House
Tower of London EC3N 4AB

Jewish Museum
Raymond Barson House
129 Albert Street NW1

Livery Companies
see 'Societies and Periodicals'

Lloyds Nelson Collection
Lloyds,
Lime Street EC3M 7HA
(By appointment only)

Museum of London
London Wall EC2Y 5HN

Museum of the Order of Saint John
St John's Lane
Clerkenwell EC1M 4DA

Museum of the Royal Mint
7 Grosvenor Gardens SW1W 0BH

National Army Museum
Royal Hospital Road
Chelsea SW3 4HT

National Maritime Museum
Romney Road
Greenwich SE10 9NF

Science Museum
Exhibition Road
South Kensington SW7 2DD

United Grand Lodge of England Library
and Museum
Freemasons' Hall
Great Street WC2B 5AZ

Victoria and Albert Museum
Cromwell Road
South Kensington SW7 2RL

Victoria and Albert Museum Archive of Art
and Design
Blythe House
23 Blythe Road W14 0QF

Wallace Collection
Hertford House
Manchester Square W1M 6BN

Wellington Museum
Apsley House
Hyde Park Corner W1V 9FA

The Rest of England

American Museum in Britain
Claverton Manor
Bath
Avon BA2 7BD

Ashmolean Museum of Art and
Archaeology
Beaumont Street
Oxford OX1 2PH

Bowes Museum
Barnard Castle
Co. Durham DL12 8NP

Birmingham City Archives
Central Library
Chamberlain Square
Birmingham B3 3HQ

Birmingham Museum and Art Gallery
Chamberlain Square
Birmingham B3 3DH

Bristol City Museum and Art Gallery
Queen's Road
Bristol BS8 1RL

Castle Museum
The Castle
Nottingham NG1 6EL

Cecil Higgins Art Gallery and Museum
Castle Close
Bedford MK40 3NY

Cheltenham Art Gallery and Museum
Clarence Street
Cheltenham GL50 3JT

Doncaster Museum and Art Gallery
Chequer Road
Doncaster DN1 2AE

Fairfax House
Castlegate
York YO1 1RN

Fitzwilliam Museum
Trumpington Street
Cambridge CB2 1RB

Grosvenor Museum
27 Grosvenor Street
Chester CH1 2DD

Jewellery Quarter Discovery Centre
77-79 Vyse Street
Hockley
Birmingham B18 6HA

Kendal Abbot Hall Art Gallery
Abbot Hall
Kendal
Cumbria lA9 5AL

Laing Art Gallery
Higham Place
Newcastle upon Tyne NE1 8AG

Leicester Museum and Art Gallery
New Walk
Leicester LE1 6TD

Liverpool Museum
William Brown Street
Liverpool L3 8EN

Lynn Museum
Market Street
King's Lynn PE30 1NL

Manchester City Art Gallery
Mosley Street
Manchester M2 3JL

Museum of North Devon
The Square
Barnstaple
Devon EX32 8LN

Newmarket Horseracing Museum
99 High Street
Newmarket
Suffolk CB8 8JL

Norwich Castle Museum
Norwich
Norfolk NR1 3JU

Plymouth City Museum and Art Gallery
Drake Circus
Plymouth PL4 8AJ

Royal Albert Memorial Museum
Queen Street
Exeter EC4 3RX

Royal Cornwall Museum
River Street
Truro
Cornwall TR1 2SJ

Royal Pavilion
4-5 Pavilion Buildings
Brighton
East Sussex BN1 1UE

Sheffield City Museum and Mappin Art
Gallery
Weston Park
Sheffield S10 2TP

Sunderland Museum and Art Gallery
Borough Road
Sunderland
Tyne and Wear SR1 1PP

Temple Newsam House
Leeds LS15 0AE

University of Liverpool Art Gallery
3 Abercromby Square
Liverpool L69 3BX

Wilberforce House
25 High Street
Hull
Humberside HU1 1EP

The Yorkshire Museum
Museum Gardens
York YO1 2DR

Ireland

National Museum of Ireland
Kildare Street
Dublin 2
Eire

Ulster Museum
Botanic Gardens
Belfast BT9 5AB

Scotland

Aberdeen Art Gallery and Museums
Schoolhill
Aberdeen AB9 1FQ

Art Galleries and Museums
Albert Square
Dundee DD1 1DA

Art Gallery and Museum
Kelvingrove
Glasgow G3 8AG

Brodick Castle Gardens and County Park
Brodick
Isle of Arran
Strathclyde KA27 8HY

Burrell Collection
2060 Pollokshaws Road
Glasgow G43 1AT

Museum and Art Gallery
Castle Wynd
Inverness IV2 3ED

National Museums of Scotland
Chambers Street
Edinburgh EH1 1 JF

Perth Museum and Art Gallery
George Street
Perth PH1 5LB

Wales

Montrose Museum and Art Gallery
Panmure Place
Montrose
Angus DD10 8HE

National Museum of Wales
Cathays Park
Cardiff CF1 3NP

Country Houses

Anglesey Abbey
Lode
Cambridgeshire CB5 9EJ

Attingham Park
Shrewsbury
Shropshire SY4 4TP

Belton House
Grantham
Lincolnshire NG32 21S

Belvoir Castle
Grantham
Lincolnshire NG32 1PD

Burghley House
Stamford
Lincolnshire PE9 3JY

Clandon Park
West Clandon
Guildford
Surrey GU4 7RQ

Dunham Massey Hall
Altrincham
Cheshire WA14 4SJ

Hampton Court Palace
East Molesey
Surrey KT8 9AU

Ickworth House
Ickworth Rotunda
Horringer
Bury St Edmunds
Suffolk IP29 5QE

Kedleston Hall
Derby DE22 5JH

Petworth House
Petworth
West Sussex GU28 OAE

Polesdon Lacey
near Dorking
Surrey RH4 1BS

Waddesdon Manor
The Rothschild Collection
Waddesdon, near Aylesbury
Bucks HP18 OJY

Woburn Abbey
Woburn
Bedfordshire MK43 0TP

Cathedral Treasuries and Church Museums

London
Saint Paul's Cathedral
Westminster Abbey
Westminster Cathedral

Bury St Edmunds
Canterbury Cathedral
Carlisle Cathedral
Chichester Cathedral
Christ Church, Oxford
Durham Cathedral
Gloucester Cathedral
Guildford Cathedral
Hereford Cathedral
Lichfield, St Mary
Lincoln Cathedral
Newark parish church
Norwich Cathedral
Norwich St Peter Mancroft
Peterborough Cathedral
Ripon Cathedral
St Albans Cathedral
Salisbury Cathedral
Winchester Cathedral
York Minster

ELSEWHERE IN EUROPE

Austria

Salzburg
Archbishop's Treasury

Vienna
Kunsthistorisches Museum und
Schatzkammer
Höfsilber und Tafelkammer
Österreichisches Museum für Angewandte
Kunst

Belgium

Brussels
Musées Royaux d'Art et d'Histoire

Bruges
Groeningenmuseum
Chateau de Seneffe
Sterckshof Silver Centre

Denmark

Copenhagen
Kunstindustrimuseet
Nationalmuseet
Fredricksborg Castle
Rosenborg Castle

France

Bordeaux
Musée des Arts Decoratifs

Paris
Louvre
Musée des Arts Decoratifs
Musée de Cluny
Musée National de la Renaissance, Ecouen

Strasbourg
Musée des Arts Decoratifs

Germany

Augsburg
Maximilianmuseum

Berlin
Kunstgewerbemuseum

Dresden
Grünes Gewölbe (Green Vaults)

Frankfurt am Main
Museum für Kunsthandwerk

Hamburg
Museum für Kunst und Gewerbe

Karlsruhe
Badisches Landesmuseum

Munich
Bayerisches Nationalmuseum
Residenz (Silberkammer and Schatzkammer)

Nuremberg
Germanisches Nationalmuseum

Stuttgart
Württembergisches Landesmuseum

Hungary

Budapest
Iparmuveszeti Museum
Magyar Nemzeti Museum

Italy

Florence
Museo degli Argenti
Palazzo Pitti

Orvieto
Museo dell'Opera del Duomo

Rome
Vatican

Siena
Museo dell'Opera del Duomo

The Netherlands

Amsterdam
Rijksmuseum
Doorn

The Hague
Gemeentemuseum

Rotterdam
Boymans-van-Beuningen Museum

Schoonhoven
Nederlands Goud-, Zilver-en Klokkenmuseum

Utrecht
Centraalmuseum

Norway

Oslo
Kunstindustrimuseet

Russia

Moscow
Kremlin
State Historical Museum

St Petersburg
State Hermitage

Spain/Portugal

Cathedral treasuries of Avila, Granada, Santiago, Saragossa, Seville, Toledo

Lisbon
Calouste Gulbenkian Foundation
Museo Nacional de Arte Antiga
Museo de Saõ Roque

Madrid
Real Academia de la Historia
Prado

Sweden

Lund
Kulturen

Stockholm
Nationalmuseum
Nordiska Museet
Royal Palace
Statens Historiska Museum

Switzerland

Basel
Historisches Museum

Zurich
Schweizerisches Landesmuseum

NORTH AMERICA

Baltimore
Walters Art Gallery

Boston
Museum of Fine Arts

Chicago
Art Institute

Williamsburg
Colonial Williamsburg

Detroit
Institute of Art

Los Angeles
County Museum of Art

Malibu
John Paul Getty Museum

Minneapolis
Institute of Art

New York
The Cloisters
Cooper Hewitt
Metropolitan Museum of Art
Museum of the City of New York

St Louis
Art Museum
Toronto
Royal Ontario Museum

Williamstown
Sterling and Francine Clark Institute

Winterthur
The Henry Francis du Pont Winterthur Museum

SOCIETIES AND PERIODICALS

UK

British Society of Enamellers
30 Kensington Square
London W8 5HH

Ephemera Society
84 Marylebone High Street
London W1

Historical Metallurgy Society
Rock House
Bowen's Hill
Coleford
Gloucester GL16 8DH

Livery Companies (City of London, visits to collections by appointment):

Clothworkers' Company
Dunster Court, 41 Mincing Lane,
London EC3R 7AH

Fishmongers' Company
London Bridge, London EC4R 9EL

Goldsmiths' Company
Foster Lane, London EC2V 6BN

Ironmongers' Company
Barbican, London EC2Y 8AA

Merchant Taylors' Company
Threadneedle Street, London EC2R 8AY

Vintner's Company
Upper Thames Street, London EC4V 3BJ

Silver Society
Secretariat
22 Orlando Road
London SW4 OLF
Periodical: The Silver Society Journal
(formerly Proceedings of the Silver Society)

Silver Spoon Club of Great Britain
Glenleigh Park
Sticker
St Austell PL26 7JB
Periodical: The Finial

Silver Study Group
PO Box 93
London NW4 3DN

Society of Jewellery Historians
(c/o The Membership Secretary)
Department of Prehistoric & Romano-
British Antiquities
The British Museum
London WC1B 3DG

Thimble Society
Stand 143 Gray's Antique Market
58 Davies Street
London W1Y 2LP

Wine Label Circle
45 Shepherds Hill
London N6 5QJ
Periodical: Journal of The Wine Label
Circle

Australia

Australian Silver Society
PO Box 142
Woollahra
Sydney 2025

Belgium

Academie von de geschiedenis von de
edelsmeetkunst in Belgie
Stathouder Braffort straat 36
1200 Brussels

Canada

Corkscrew Society
Secretary
4201 Sunflower Drive
Mississaugua
Ontario L5L2L4

Germany

Deutsches Goldschmiedehaus
Altstadter Markt 6
D-6450 Hanau

The Netherlands

The Dutch Silver Club
Van Hardenbroecklaan 19
3S32 CK Leusden
The Netherlands

USA

American Silver Guild
10812 Larkmeade Lane
Potomac. MD 20854

New York Silver Society
PO Box 1201
Madison Square Station
New York 10159-1201

Washington DC Silver Society
PO Box 5887
Washington DC 20016

Magazines

Magazines on the arts and antiques such as *Apollo, Antique Collector, Burlington Magazine, Country Life, Kunst und Antiquitaten* and *L'objet d'art* publish silver-related articles from time to time. Specialist magazines include *The Silver Magazine* (PO Box 9690, Rancho Santa Fe, CA 92067, USA) and, for a history of eating, *Petits Propos Culinaires* (Prospect Books Ltd, 45 Lamont Road, London SW10 0HU).

INDEX

A GROUPE OF THE RA